AF354268

Oscar Jewell Harvey

The Spanish Influenza Pandemic of 1918: How the US Reacted

e-artnow 2020

Oscar Jewell Harvey

The Spanish Influenza Pandemic of 1918: How the US Reacted

Efforts Made to Combat and Subdue the Disease in Luzerne County, Pennsylvania

e-artnow, 2020
Contact: info@e-artnow.org

ISBN 978-80-273-0808-8

EARLY in September, 1918, the United States was invaded by a scourge of highly infectious and fatal disease, which spread with rapidity throughout the country. It was pandemic in its nature, and partook of many of the characteristics of influenza, grip and pneumonia. No one seemed to know much about the disease or its treatment, and medical science and public health agencies were alike unprepared to cope with it.

About all that could be done at the start was to adopt and attempt to enforce drastic regulations to minimize contagion; but even in view of these regulations, and when the plague had burst forth in all its widespread malignity, the country at large seemed slow to awaken to the enormity of the peril which it faced.

It certainly was a disconcerting fact that, at the very time when vast numbers of the people in widely-distributed localities had organized themselves, through the Red Cross and other well known and efficient mediums, to fight disease and prevent suffering and death, we should be smitten with a visitation which caused more casualties and deaths among the peaceful citizens in the homeland than the deadly missiles and poisonous gases of the enemy effected among the American Expeditionary Forces overseas in the great World War.

From September 9 to November 9, according to reports received by the Federal Census Bureau from forty-six large cities in the United States having a combined population of 23,000,000 souls, there was a total of 82,306 deaths attributed to the scourge. In a similar period of time, in the same communities, the normal number of deaths dues to influenza and pneumonia would have been about 4,000.

In the latter part of September 85,000 cases in Massachusetts alone were reported; and by the first week in October the disease was prevalent in nearly all sections of the United States — twenty-three States, from Massachusetts in the East to California in the West, and from Florida in the South-east to Washington in the North-west, were experiencing the mysterious malady. More than 14,000 cases in the military camps of the country were reported to the office of the Surgeon General of the Army within one period of twenty-four hours.

Up to January 4, 1919, according to the Census Bureau, the mortality due to the fatal disease was 115,258 in forty-six cities of the United States containing one-fifth of the population of the country; while, according to statistics submitted to the Actuarial Society of America in July, 1919, 450,000 deaths occurred in the United States in the Autumn and early Winter of 1918 due to this pandemic disease-which wrought its greatest havoc among infants and persons in adult working life. The mortality of males was greater than that of females, while the highest mortality caused by the disease affected persons of the wage-earning class-especially those situated in the lowest economic range.

The origin or source of the disease was unknown. Some experts looked upon it as simply a variety of a well-known disease prevalent, with occasional outbreaks of violence, for hundreds of years. Others attempted to identify it with a form of pneumonic plague that has raged in parts of China for a number of years past-China and its neighboring lands in Asia forming a vast storehouse of infection from which great epidemics have swept in waves across and around the globe.

It is an historic fact that, in the early part of 1917 about 200,000 coolies, collected from the northern part of China (where the pneumonic plague had raged for six or seven years), were sent to France as laborers, and with them went the germs of the pneumonic plague. Many of these coolies were captured by the Germans in the Spring of 1918 —hence the outbreak of the plague, at that time, in the German army, where it is said to have been very serious in its deadly character.

There were some writers of the press who declared that the disease had been brought into this country in German submarine boats; but when it was realized that, like a scourge of the Middle Ages, it was sweeping through Europe-no part of which, civilized or barbarian, was exempt-it was called by many experts a by-product of the World War.

The manner of the pandemic's appearance in different countries indicated that the germs of the disease had been conveyed thither by the currents of the air. Therefore the theory was broached, that the poison gases, with which many sectors of the fighting area in Europe and Asia were drenched, were carried by the winds in every direction, causing the outbreak of the pandemic in England, Germany, France, Spain, Australia, Africa and Asia, as well as in North America and some of the South American countries.

The disease took its deadly toll even in lonely Labrador, in the "silent North" of the Western Hemisphere, where ice-floes from farther north fill every harbor of the rock-bound coast; where giant icebergs, miles in length, mountains in height and acres in extent bar the paths of ships and steamers. "A land where railroads are unknown, where streets are never laid nor roads built to connect one settlement with another; a country where horses and cows are less known than are the rhinoceros and zebra to the inhabitants of the United States; a region where even canned milk is a luxury and candy is seldom seen."

On all the desolate coast of Labrador, extending over eight degrees of latitude, not a doctor nor a trained nurse, not a hospital nor a dispensary, not even a health officer, was to be found. Eskimo and Indian, German and Briton, halfbreed and white, hunter and fisherman, fell victims to the dreaded scourge, which traveled with rapidity. Whole settlements were left without a single survivor-the unburied corpses being devoured by halfstarved dogs. This is the story that came out of the "silent North" —the most gruesome, most awful, tale of disease and death that the world has heard in many a day!

Following the outbreak of the scourge in Germany it was next heard of in Spain, where it received the name "Spanish influenza". This is really a misnomer, but it has stuck, probably because the disease to which it was applied was the first epidemic of influenza Spain had ever experienced. This name accompanied the disease to the United States, where, by some slangologists, it was early transmogrified into "flu" —by which appellation it has been pretty commonly designated.

The scourge invaded Pennsylvania about the middle of September, 1918, simultaneously attacking widely-separated communities. On October 1 the Department of Health of the Commonwealth issued orders directing the closing of all moving picture houses, theaters and places of amusement in general; that public assemblages be discontinued; that funerals be privately conducted; that all bar-rooms and wholesale liquor establishments be closed. The matter of closing schools, churches and Sunday schools was left to the discretion of local authorities. In addition, the Department issued proclamations and appeals for hearty co-operation on the part of the general public in checking the ravages of the scourge.

In Wilkes-Barre on October 3, 4 and 5 the directions and appeals of the State Department of Health were promptly and cheerfully compiled with (even clubs and the various fraternal orders and societies observing the mandates, while the sessions of the Courts of Luzerne County for the week beginning October 7 were continued and postponed), although on the first day of the appearance of the disease here only twenty cases were officially reported.

Owing to the absence of many local physicians and trained nurses in the military and naval services of the United States, Wyoming Valley Chapter of the Red Cross issued an appeal on October 3 for trained nurses and for women with some nursing experience to register with the Chapter for service in combating the disease here.

Under the date of October 8 the Commissioner of Health of Pennsylvania issued a circular letter to Department of Health and other physicians "engaged in the State-wide organization against the Influenza Epidemic," in which, among other things, the following information and instructions were set forth:

"From close observation of the progress of the pandemic of influenza which is now sweeping upon us from the Atlantic seaboard, it has been decided by the Governor of this Commonwealth, the Commissioner of Health and the Advisory Board of the Pennsylvania Department of Health to use the organization at hand, and all available organizations that will co-operate to the utmost, in an effort to save the lives of our people. Accordingly, after careful thought, the following [among other] plans have been adopted:

"The State Department of Health to be in absolute control and take full responsibility.

"The formation of nineteen Epidemic Emergency Districts, with a representative of the Department in full charge of each district, taking his orders directly from the Commissioner of Health and transmitting them to those who answer the call.

"Appeals to all Health, Patriotic, Civic, Religious, Business and Social organizations, such as the Red Cross (graduates in elementary hygiene and home care of the sick, or first aid). Associated Charities, Boards of Health, Mayors, Councils, County Commissioners, Directors of the Poor, Boards of Trade, Church Societies, Fraternal Orders, Women's Clubs, Boy Scouts, Motor Messenger Corps, trained nurses, practical attendants, lay workers and volunteer automobilists, to lend all possible assistance under the direction of the Department.

"The Adjutant General has placed the entire State Guard, and all the equipment of his department, at our disposal for the erection of emergency hospitals, furnishing of supplies, safe-guarding of property and the maintenance of discipline.

"Requests for aid from stricken communities should be made to the nearest representative of the Department, who will refer them to the physician in charge of the Epidemic Emergency District. This includes calls for doctors, nurses, aids, materials and any other form of relief. The Department will make a supreme effort to satisfy all such needs as rapidly as possible. However, where these are at hand, they should be obtained locally. * * *

"All attendants should wear masks. * * *

"Treatment of Influenza and Pneumonia. * * *"

In furthering the foregoing plans and regulations Dr. Charles H. Miner of Wilkes-Barre, who was at that time, and had been for ten years, County Medical Inspector of the State Department of Health for Luzerne County, was appointed on October 8, by the Acting Commissioner of Health (Dr. B. Franklin Royer), "to take full charge of the organization and co-ordination of all work in District No. 5," composed of Luzerne and Columbia Counties, with headquarters at Wilkes-Barre.

The same day the Acting Commissioner telephoned from Harrisburg to the County Medical Inspector at Wilkes-Barre, informing the latter of his appointment as aforementioned, and asking him to request Maj. Gen. C. B. Dougherty of Wilkes-Barre to aid him in arranging and setting forward plans for the proper handling of the situation in the 5th District.

General Dougherty responded promptly to the call for his services, and he and the County Medical Inspector soon concluded, in view of the fact that the regular and permanent hospitals located in the 5th District were just about "crowded to their limits" with influenza and pneumonic patients, and that the new cases reported each day in the various communities were becoming more numerous, that it would be necessary to establish and equip several emergency hospitals.

It was decided to establish an Emergency Hospital in Wilkes Barre (where, on October 8, sixty new cases of influenza had been reported to the County Medical Inspector), and the armory of the 9th Regiment, National Guard of Pennsylvania, located on South Main Street, was selected for the purpose.

For some time then the 2d Infantry, Pennsylvania Reserve Militia (Col. S. E. W. Eyer commanding), had occupied the armory as its headquarters. On October 8 Colonel Eyer turned over the armory to the representatives of the Department of Health, and immediately, under the direction and supervision of General Dougherty, the work of thoroughly scrubbing and cleaning the building from top to bottom was begun and was rapidly completed. Then the Shepherd Construction Company of Wilkes Barre began the erection of four wards on the drill floor of the armory.

Each of these wards was 21x27 feet in area by 10 feet in height, the walls, or partitions, being constructed of hemlock studding covered with beaver board. Each ward had a capacity of fifteen cots,[1] whereby ample air space was allowed for each patient. Considerable plumbing work had to be installed in order to facilitate the efforts of nurses and attendants in giving proper care and attention to the hospital patients. This plumbing work, when completed, represented an outlay of $605.49. Also, the lighting facilities of the armory not being sufficient, it was necessary to install additional wiring and lights throughout the entire building, which was done at an expense of $190.

The basement of the armory was transformed into a commodious and comfortable dining-room; the kitchen was painted white, made sanitary in every respect, and its floor was covered with oil-cloth, while gas ranges were connected and refrigerators were installed. A diet kitchen (separate from the main kitchen) was established convenient to the main floor of the armory.

On the evening of October 9, upon invitation of the County Medical Inspector, the following-named ladies and gentlemen assembled in the auditorium of the Wilkes-Barre Chamber of Commerce, "for the purpose of taking steps for combating influenza": Dr. Charles H. Miner, Dr. S. P. Mengel, Dr. G. A. Clark, Dr. E. L. Meyers, Dr. Charles Long, Gen. C. B. Dougherty, Col. S. E. W. Eyer, Lewis P. Kniffen, E. E. Matthews, Anthony C. Campbell, M. J. McLaughhn, John D. Farnham, M. H. Sigafoos, Maj. E. N. Carpenter, William H. Conyngham, Frederick E. Zerbey, George J. Hartman, Hayden Williams, Mrs. C. H. Miner, Mrs. E. Birney Carr and Miss Josephine Tracy of Wilkes-Barre; Dr. W. B. Strieker, Dr. J. Hughes, Michael Douk, T. A. Butkiewicz, C. J. Donahey, John Badman and F. H. Kohlbraker of Nanticoke; R. Alvan Beisel of Hazleton; Mrs. W. A. Lathrop of Dorranceton; Dr. J. A. Hilbert, Miss Esther J. Tinsley, Dr. S. L. Underwood and William J. Peck of Pittston; R. A. Mulhall of West Pittston; Dr. S. B. Arment of Bloomsburg; Dr. D. H. Lake, S. H. Hicks and W. B. Crane of Kingston.

General Dougherty was called upon to preside, and Hayden Williams, Secretary of the Chamber of Commerce, acted as Secretary of the meeting.

The County Medical Inspector spoke at great length with respect to the work already done in the 5th District to combat the pandemic-referring particularly to the emergency hospital which had been established at Wanamie, in Newport Township, Luzerne County, and to the preparations being made for the opening of the Armory Emergency Hospital in Wilkes-Barre. He stated that he had divided the 5th District into five sub-districts, with Dr. S. B. Arment in charge of the work in Columbia County, Dr. J. W. Leckie in charge of the Hazleton sub-district, Dr. W. B. Strieker in charge of a district extending from Nanticoke south to the Columbia County line. Dr. S. L. Underwood in charge of a district extending from the borough of Wyoming to the Lackawanna County line, while he, himself, in addition to a general supervision of affairs in the 5th District, had assumed charge of the work in the territory extending from Wyoming to Nanticoke. He suggested that committees on automobiles, food, drugs and general hospital supplies should be appointed.

General Dougherty gave an account of the serious conditions existing at Minersville and Shamokin in the 3d District, adjoining the 5th District. Dr. Underwood and Miss Tinsley spoke of conditions in Exeter, Luzerne County, where nearly 300 cases then existed. They reported that there were 182 cases in 62 homes; that 98 patients were convalescing; that 10 families were in dire need of help, and that there was a special urgency for women to help in the house-work of afflicted families.

Dr. Hughes said that there were 400 cases at Glen Lyon and Wanamie in Newport Township; that sanitary conditions were bad; that there was a lack of nurses, and that the high-school building at Wanamie had just been converted into an emergency hospital.

Dr. G. A. Clark, head of the Wilkes-Barre City Health Department, stated that about 200 cases had been reported in the city, and that the municipality would bear its proper share of the expense incurred in efforts to check the disease.

Dr. Lake stated that there were 36 cases in Kingston and 40 in Edwardsville, and that there had been two or three deaths from the disease. In one home in Edwardsville there were seven cases. He declared that the closing of the schools had helped somewhat in checking the spread of the disease, and that considerable good could be accomplished if Toby's Creek, which had never been cleaned, were placed in a sanitary condition.

Dr. Arment stated that conditions in Catawissa, Columbia County, were bad; that a hospital was needed there, but it was impossible to procure nurses. Six deaths had occurred thus far in that locality, and the disease seemed to be spreading. He suggested that the school-houses in Bloomsburg be converted into emergency hospitals, and reported that the saloons in Centralia were wide open and doing business as usual.

W. H. Conyngham, representing Wyoming Valley Chapter of the American Red Cross, stated that his organization had no funds with which to pay nurses, but that the members of the Chapter stood ready to do anything in their power to combat the disease.

Dr. Mengel, Chief Surgeon of The Lehigh Valley Coal Company, placed the nurses of that organization at the disposal of the community, and suggested that school teachers should be employed to help in the work of caring for the sick.

Mrs. E. Birney Carr reported that the Canteen Service of the Wyoming Valley Chapter of the Red Cross would render all the assistance possible, while Mr. McLaughlin, one of the Commissioners of Luzerne County, gave assurance that the County would render any assistance possible to help stamp out the disease

The Secretary of the Wilkes-Barre Chamber of Commerce volunteered the assistance of the Chamber's staff in handling all details of the work connected with the campaign. Dr. Charles Long suggested that an effort be made to secure financial and other assistance from the Board of Directors of the Central Poor District of Luzerne County.

Anthony C. Campbell, Esq., County Fuel Administrator, told of the serious conditions with respect to the mining industry in the 5th District, and declared that the output of anthracite coal was being seriously affected by the pandemic. On motion of Mr. Campbell it was then unanimously voted: That such emergency hospitals as the County Medical Inspector deemed necessary be established, that those in charge of the work incident to combating the influenza-pneumonia scourge should call upon the Board of Directors of the Central Poor District, County officials and the various municipal officers in the 5th District for financial assistance in defraying such expenses as may be necessarily incurred in carrying on their work, and that the County Medical Inspector be given any and all assistance required.

The meeting then adjourned, and within a day or two thereafter the County Medical Inspector announced the appointment of various committees "to cooperate with the State Department of Health in the 5th District with respect to the influenza epidemic," as follows:

General Committee. —To have general supervision over the hospitals established. To provide ways and means, and secure appropriations and financial aid from the several municipalities. All funds raised, except State funds, to be placed in the hands of the Treasurer of the General Committee. All expenditures to be approved by the General Committee and its Chairman.

Maj. Gen. C. B. Dougherty (representing the Susquehanna Collieries Co.), Chairman; Hayden Williams (representing the Chamber of Commerce), Secretary; M. J. McLaughlin (County Commissioner), Wm. H. Conyngham (Red Cross), Lewis P. Kniffen (City Council), R. Nelson Bennett (City Council), Wm. C. Shepherd (Chamber of Commerce), J. L. Reilly (Central Poor District), Dr. S. P. Mengel (Lehigh Valley Coal Co.), Dr. G. A. Clark (City Health Board), Dr. E. L. Meyers (School Board), Miss Mary Trescott (School Board), F. H. Kohlbraker (Susquehanna Collieries Co.), Dr. J. W. Geist (Lehigh and Wilkes-Barre Coal Co.), Frederick E. Zerbey (Kingston Coal Co.), Samuel T. Nicholson (Vulcan Iron Works), M. H. Sigafoos (Hazard Manufacturing Co.), Fred. H. Gates (City Clerk), and Fuller R. Hendershot (County Controller).

Emergency Hospital Committee. —This committee to have general charge of the establishment of emergency hospitals and direct their conduct and care, including arrangements for and maintenance of subsistence for patients and help.

Dr. S. P. Mengel of Wilkes-Barre, Chairman; Drs. Lewis H. Taylor, W. S. Stewart and L. A. Sheridan of Wilkes-Barre, Dr. Cohen of Berwick, Dr. H. B. Wilcox of Kingston, Dr. H. Whitney of Plymouth, Dr. H. J. Lenahan of Pittston, Dr. Jesse Hughes of Nanticoke, Dr. J. H. Bruner of Bloomsburg, and Dr. Walter Lathrop of Hazleton.

Canteen Relief Committee. —This committee to have charge of the preparation of food, and the preparation of the same for transportation to outside patients at their homes-this transportation to be provided by the Motor Transportation Committee.

The ladies of the Red Cross Canteen Service are to compose this Relief Committee, with Mrs. E. Birney Carr as Chairman.

Armory Hospital Committee. —This committee, under the direction of the Emergency Hospital Committee, to have charge of the care and maintenance of sanitary conditions of the Armory, and to provide for the disposal of refuse.

Col. S. E. W. Eyer, Chairman; Capt. Robert R. Harvey, Lieut. Charles E. Trein, Lieut. Robert D. Raeder, Harry W. French, and Wayne Canfield.

The medical staff for the Armory Hospital to consist of: Drs. W. Clive Smith, D. S. Kistler, Parke Sickler, Charles Long, John T. Howell, Allan C. Brooks, E. J. Flanagan, J. B. Tobias, Maurice B. Ahlborn, Herbert B. Gibby and Walter B. Foss, and their duties being to act as aids to the Superintendent of the Emergency Hospital, and to accept assignments for service from time to time as the demands may require-the schedule of this service to be arranged by the Chairman of the Emergency Hospital Committee, with a minimum demand on the time of the Staff Physicians, and only as the exigencies required.

Motor Transportation Committee. —This committee to have charge of the motor transportation for the transfer of nurses from hospitals and patients to and from the homes of the sick. Under this committee a sub-committee of men to be organized to arrange for the transportation of food to homes.

Mrs. W. A. Lathrop, Chairman; Mrs. Lawrence B. Jones, Mrs. Robert A. Quin, Miss Caroline Marcy, Stephen Pettebone and Frank F. Matheson.

Nurses' Aid Committee. —This committee to have charge of the selection and recruiting of all trained nurses, Red Cross nurses and volunteer nurses for the Emergency Hospitals, and visiting nurses for homes.

Mrs. Charles H. Miner, Chairman; Mrs. J. Pryor Williamson, Mrs. Charles P. Elliott, Mrs. Paul Bedford, Mrs. Wm. H. Conyngham, Mrs. Charles P. Hunt, Mrs. E. Byron Strome, Mrs. E. B. Wagner, Miss C. L. Best, Miss Ethel Sturdevant, Miss Margaret Bevans, Miss Georgia Grossman, Miss Clara Treglawn, Miss Ruth Williams, Miss Corrigan, Miss Ruth Benscoter and Miss Isabelle Cairns.

Drug Store Committee. —This committee to organize the drug stores, and have them provide and keep in stock such medicines and medical goods as will be required for the Emergency Hospitals. Also, to secure and provide a stock of drugs and supplies for the Emergency Hospitals.

Louis Frank, Chairman; Edward H. White, Lieut. Charles E, Trein and Henry W. Merritt.

Luzerne County Cooperation Committee-This committee, representing the municipal governments and the Boards of Health in their respective districts, to cooperate with the General Committee by organizing in their towns a house to house census, and report all cases of influenza and sickness to the Chairman of the General Committee, and to aid and cooperate in every way to prevent the spread of the disease. This committee to be subject to the call of the General Committee for conference, as well as the other committees. Community Captains to report to Community Chairmen, the latter to report to District Chairmen, and they to report daily to the General Chairman of the Cooperation Committee. The latter to report daily to Dr. Miner, representing the State Department of Health.

Percy A. Brown, Wilkes-Barre, General Chairman; Hayden Williams, Wilkes-Barre, General Secretary; Dr. Joseph Dougherty and Frank McQuown, Ashley; William G. Rowett and CHfford Edwards, Courtdale; Louis Jacobs and William Mundy, Exeter; William Evans and William A. Wallace, Forty Fort; Dr. D. H. Lake and Rush Trescott, Kingston; John Doran and Edward Lawler, Larksville; George Knarr and R. J. Blair, Luzerne ; Dr. F. E. Davis and William Oldfield, Nanticoke; O. O. Eisenhower and Harry Brown, Dorranceton; James Doran, Parsons; Dr. H. Templeton and George E. Gwilliam, Plymouth, and Dr. Milton Barton, Plains.

General Headquarters-Greater Wilkes-Barre Chamber of Commerce, Miners Bank Building, Wilkes-Barre.

Luzerne County District Chairmen. —District No. i, Henry W. Ruggles, Dorranceton; District No. 2, H. L. Freeman, Plymouth ; District No. 3, G. D. Stroh, West Pittston; District No. 4, Joseph M. Stark, Hudson; District No. 5, Rev. F. Kasaczun, Sugar Notch; District No. 6, E. B. Wesley, Nanticoke; District No. 7, Harry A. Schmoll, Hazleton.

District No. 1, composed of the boroughs and hamlets of Courtdale, Dallas, Dorranceton, Exeter, Forty Fort, Kingston, Luzerne, Pringle, Shavertown, Swoyerville, Trucksville, West Pittston, Wyoming and West Wyoming, and the townships of Kingston, Franklin, Exeter and Dallas.

District No. 2, composed of the boroughs of Edwardsville, Larksville, Plymouth and Shickshinny, and the townships of Fairmount, Hunlock, Huntington, Jackson, Lake, Lehman, Plymouth, Ross, Salem and Union.

District No. 3, composed of the city and township of Pittston, and the boroughs of Avoca, Dupont, Duryea and Hughestown.

District No. 4, composed of the boroughs of Laflin, Miner's Mills, Parsons and Yatesville, and the townships of Jenkins and Plains.

District No. 5, composed of the boroughs of Ashley, Laurel Run, Nuangola, Sugar Notch and Warrior Run, and the townships of Wilkes-Barre, Fairview, Bear Creek, Buck, Wright, Slocum and Denison.

District No. 6, composed of the borough of Nanticoke, the village of Macanaqua, the borough and township of Nescopeck, and the townships of Conyngham, Dorrance, Hollenback, Newport and Slocum.

District No. 7, composed of the city of Hazleton and all territory contiguous thereto.

The following rules, governing the "operation of community organizations and the duties of each organization unit," were promulgated:

"1. Community Chairman. —Shall act as Chairman of the Executive Committee and be responsible for the operation of each unit. Receive reports daily from all subordinates, and report daily to the Chairman of the District in which the community is situated.

"2. Executive Committee. —To meet and work only under direction of the Community Chairman. This committee shall assist the Community Chairman in carrying out all rules and regulations.

"3. Secretary. —To have some one constantly on duty at the Emergency Station. Keep a record of all cases and any other information required. Prepare a daily report for Community Chairman, also receive all calls for nurses, canteen service, medical attention when physicians are overworked, and be in a position at all times to furnish accurate information. It is preferred that a school teacher be engaged to assist the Secretary.

"4, Emergency Station. —To be centrally and conveniently located. To be equipped with a telephone for use by the Secretary and other officials. To be open during business hours.

"5. Community Captains. —Under the direction of the Community Chairman and Executive Committee a Captain shall be appointed for each community. In case of an unusually long street, the number of Captains for said street may be increased. Captains will make a daily tour of their streets, and report daily to the Community Chairman, through the Secretary at the Emergency Station, the number of new cases, deaths and discharged cases. Captains will also note sanitary conditions and conditions in general, and aid in eliminating any condition that may cause a spread of disease. Captains will also report any cases needing medical attention or a nurse.

"6. Nursing Bureau. —To be located at the Emergency Station and be under the direction of Red Cross workers. Here a record should be kept of every woman who volunteers as a nurse or nurse's assistant. From this Bureau should also be supplied gowns and masks to protect nurses when they go into the homes of the sick.

"7. Canteen Service. —To distribute food for the sick in homes where food is needed. Care should be exercised to see that this service is not abused. The Canteen should be established preferably in a church kitchen, and here should be prepared soup or broth to be distributed in jars or pails to the doors of the homes from which calls have been received.

"8. Automobile Service. —Secure one car or truck daily for service at the Canteen, and other machines to carry nurses and physicians to homes of patients when necessary.

"9. Publicity Bureau. —To assume charge of distributing leaflets in different languages, disseminate general information, and assist through publicity in bringing about enforcement of all health regulations.

"MISCELLANEOUS GENERAL INSTRUCTIONS.

"Impress every member of the community organization with the seriousness of the situation, and make each one responsible toward having people obey all instructions.

"Remember that it is easier to prevent an epidemic than to stop one when conditions become dangerous.

"Don't frighten people about the situation, but constantly prevail upon them to be careful in not exposing themselves to disease or spreading it.

"Permit no public gatherings or large groups on street corners, in stores, etc.

"Permit no public funerals, and have a police or health officer attend all funerals to enforce the law in this respect. "Let 'Safety First' be the motto of all people.

"It is especially requested that all schools and churches be closed."

In pursuance of the resolution adopted at the meeting held in the Chamber of Commerce on October 9, as aforementioned, Dr. Miner gave directions for the establishing of emergency hospitals at the following-named places-in addition to those already arranged for at Wanamie and in the Armory at Wilkes-Barre: Catawissa, Exeter, Hazleton, Dupont, Nanticoke and Plains.[2]

On October 10 the first emergency hospital was opened, in the Central High School building at Wanamie, with Dr. William H. Corrigan physician in charge and Miss Emily G. Jones, Graduate Nurse, as chief nurse. The same day the emergency hospital at Catawissa was opened, with Dr. S. B. Arment physician in charge and Miss Hannah C. Breisch, Graduate Nurse, as chief nurse. On October 11 the third emergency hospital was opened, in the High School building at Exeter, with Dr. James Dixon physician in charge and Miss Jessie Cunningham and Mrs. Ernest W. Hogg, Graduate Nurses, as chief nurses.

Dr. Elmer L. Hinman, having been sent to Wilkes-Barre by Dr. Royal S. Copeland, Commissioner of the Health Department of the city of New York, reported to the County Medical Inspector for duty on October 12, and was assigned to the Wanamie Emergency Hospital to assist Dr. Corrigan.

At this time it was estimated that there were at least 1,000 influenza and pneumonia cases, reported and unreported, in Wilkes-Bar re-new cases appearing at the rate of nearly 100 per day. The Wilkes-Barre City Hospital refused, because of lack of room and nurses, to receive any more cases. Nurses and doctors everywhere were overworked, and the situation at Glen Lyon (in Newport Township) and in Hazleton and its vicinity was appalling.

In the afternoon of October 12 a meeting of Chairmen of committees and Division Chairman was held with the County Medical Inspector at the rooms of the Chamber of Commerce, when it was decided that trucks should be secured for the purpose of delivering food daily to the homes of the sick, where such service was needed. Whereupon Percy A. Brown and Frank F. Matheson each offered trucks for this purpose. It was suggested that Mrs. P. J. Higgins of Wilkes-Barre should be placed in charge of the cooking at the Armory canteen-the necessary arrangements for this service, however, to be left in the hands of the Canteen Committee.

Dr. Mengel suggested that a telegram be sent to the proper authorities at Washington, urging them to leave here, during the progress of the epidemic, all Red Cross nurses now in this vicinity. General Dougherty reported that he had communicated with the Hon. A. Mitchell Palmer and other Government officials at Washington relative to having army surgeons sent here from

16

Camp Crane, Allentown, Pennsylvania, and he had been assured that ten officers of the Medical Department would be sent.

Dr. S. M. Wolfe of Wilkes-Barre, who had recently returned from Massachusetts, where he had assisted in combating the epidemic, told of the various organized methods and plans pursued in dealing with the disease in that State.

Mr. William J, Ruff, Cashier of the Luzerne County National Bank, Wilkes-Barre, was then elected Treasurer of the General Committee.

At the close of this meeting General Dougherty telegraphed to Maj. Gen. Rupert Blue, Surgeon General, U. S. A., Dr. H. A.

Garfield, U. S. Fuel Administrator, and Miss Carrie Noyes, Director of Field Nursing, American Red Cross, at Washington, D. C, as follows:

"The following Red Cross nurses have been called to leave for service on Tuesday, October 15: Miss Edith Evans, Miss Elsie Banker and Mrs. Lena Krum of Wilkes-Barre; Miss Hazel Smith of Tunkhannock, Pa., and Miss Bessie Evans of Kingston, Pa. The influenza situation in Wyoming Valley is of such a serious nature, and there is such a dearth of nurses, that, as Chairman of the General Committee of Wyoming Valley (whose efforts are being directed toward the stamping out of this pestilence, in order to conserve the lives of our citizens and thus maintain the production of anthracite coal, which is now seriously affected by the prevailing sickness), I appeal to you to direct these nurses to remain here to take up their duties in emergency hospitals now being established. I trust that this appeal will be fully appreciated by you. We are fearfully short of nurses as well as doctors. We can use a great many physicians and nurses."

On October 13 the following-named medical officers from Camp Crane arrived at Wilkes-Barre, and were assigned to duty by Dr. Miner, as noted: Capt. E. L. Hendricks, U. S. Marine Corps, and Lieut. C. F. Bahler, to Glen Lyon; Lieut. Joseph Goldstone, U. S. Marine Corps, to Bloomsburg; Lieut. G. T. Meek to Exeter, and Lieut. J. A. M. Aspy to Hazleton,

At a meeting of the General Committee held in the auditorium of the Chamber of Commerce on Tuesday, October 15, General Dougherty presented a report relative to conditions at Shamokin and Minersville (in the 3d District), where there were 4,000 cases of the "flu". Col. Eyer reported on the work being done at the Armory to fit it for hospital purposes, and Dr. Miner stated that the Armory Emergency Hospital would be ready for the reception of patients at noon on the following day.

The Rev. John J. McCabe, of St. Joseph's R. C. Church, Georgetown, told of conditions in Wilkes-Barre Township, where, he said, there were 80 cases of the disease. Dr. Hughes stated that there were about 585 cases in Newport Township and vicinity, and Richard Sheridan reported that there were possibly over 200 cases in Nanticoke.

On motion of the Rev. Mr. McCabe the Chairman named Dr. C. H. Miner, the Rev. J. F. Jedlicka and Dr. E. L. Meyers as a committee to confer with the Controller and Commissioners of Luzerne County, and the Directors of the Central Poor District, for the purpose of securing financial aid in fighting the epidemic. Controller Hendershot, who was present, stated that he would do everything in his power to co-operate with the General Committee in its work. James L. Reilly, Secretary of the Central District Poor Board, who was present, stated that he felt sure the Poor Board would co-operate with the Committee.

Frederick E. Zerbey, Superintendent of the Kingston Coal Company, offered the use of the ambulances of that company to convey patients from the west side of the river.

General Dougherty stated that the State would pay for doctors, nurses, tents, cots, blankets, sheets, etc., employed and used in combating the epidemic, but that all other service would have to be paid for with funds derived from other sources.

On October 16 the Hazleton Emergency Hospital was opened in the building of St. Gabriel's High School, Hazleton, with Lieut. J. A. M. Aspy physician in charge and Miss Ruth B. Rae, Graduate Nurse, from the Department of Health, as chief nurse. (Later, Miss Rae was stricken with the "flu" and was succeeded as chief nurse by the Mother Superior of St. Gabriel's, who was a professional nurse. On October 25 Lieutenant Aspy returned to Camp Crane, and was succeeded by Dr. J. W. Leckie as physician in charge at Hazleton.)

On October 12 the Armory Emergency Hospital at Wilkes Barre was ready with four wards for the reception of patients. Lack of nurses, however, delayed the opening of the hospital until Wednesday, October 16, when, with Capt. E. L. Hendricks, U. S. M. C, as physician in charge, and Mrs. J. Pryor Williamson of Wilkes-Barre, Graduate Nurse, as chief nurse, the doors were opened at one o'clock p. m. for the reception of patients. During the afternoon six female and five male patients from Wilkes-Barre, Nanticoke, Parsons and Miner's Mills were received, and on the following day eleven males and seven females were received from Wilkes-Barre, Edwardsville, Plymouth, Miner's Mills, Maltby, Nanticoke and Forty Fort.

The sixth Emergency Hospital in the 5th District was opened on October 17 in the Pulaski School building at Dupont, Luzerne County, with Dr. W. S. Helman of Avoca as visiting physician and Miss Herman, Graduate Nurse, as chief nurse. (Dr. Helman was succeeded on November 9 by Dr. James S. Dixon, and Miss Herman was succeeded on November 19 by Miss Bessie Fadden.)

The seventh Emergency Hospital was opened on October 17 m the Washington School building at Nanticoke, Luzerne County, with Dr. Elmer L. Hinman in charge and Miss Olwen Williams, Graduate Nurse, as chief nurse. (Dr. Hinman returned to New York City on October 26, and was succeeded by Lieut. C. E. Yates.)

On October 17 two medical students, Messrs. J. A. Post and W. R. Stewart, of the University of Buffalo, reported to the County Medical Inspector at Wilkes-Barre to help out with the work of the 5th District. Mr. Stewart was assigned to assist Dr. Corrigan at the Wanamie Hospital, and Mr. Post was assigned to the Exeter, and subsequently to the Plains, Emergency Hospital.

The same day the following-named Army Surgeons arrived at Wilkes-Barre and were assigned to the Hazleton District: Captains Davenport and Danfort to work at Jeddo; Captain Brown at Cranberry; Captain Wroth at Lattimer and Major Wyer in Hazleton. On October 19, however, all these Surgeons were offered to return to Camp Crane, Allentown.

On October 18 a largely-attended meeting of the General Committee was held, with General Dougherty, Chairman, presiding. The latter outlined the objects and purposes in view with respect to the emergency hospitals which had been established, stating that only patients who could not receive proper attention at their homes should be sent to the hospitals. He also set forth the fact that there was a very great shortage of doctors and nurses in this District, and called upon Miss Nellie G. Loftus, the State nurse in charge of the nurses in this section, to make a statement as to conditions here. This she did, setting forth that there were thirty graduate nurses in the 5th District, five or six of whom were not in active service on account of illness. There were also eleven practical nurses in the District, but at least fifty more graduate nurses could, and should, be placed in service immediately.

Mr. W. C. Shepherd then made the following motion, which was adopted:

"It is the sense of this meeting that all patriotic citizens will, in every case where possible so to do, release nurses from their private employ for the general good of the community. It is their patriotic duty to do this during the present grave emergency."

Mr. Percy A. Brown, Chairman of the Co-operation Committee, stated that the territory in Luzerne County had been divided into forty sub-districts, and that he had arranged to have an organization in each sub-district. Thirty-two of the forty organizations had already reported to him. He suggested that leaflets, containing brief and simple rules for avoiding influenza and for the care of the sick, be printed in several foreign languages, and widely distributed.[3]

Mr. Brown also suggested that a fund be created from which money could be drawn to be used in paying some one in each subdistrict to look after and report upon the sanitary and health conditions in that particular locality.

Anthony C. Campbell, Esq., Fuel Administrator for this section of the State, stated that he had received reports from various large coal-mining companies, which had enabled him to prepare a statement showing that from 28,000 to 30,000 tons of coal had been lost to the industry on account of the influenza.

On motion of Mr. W. C. Shepherd it was voted that all communities in this District be requested to organize committees on the plan endorsed or recommended by the State Board of Health. In pursuance of this motion Chairman Dougherty appointed Wm. C. Shepherd, Dr. Charles H. Miner, Dr. S. P. Mengel, Dr. E. L. Meyers, A. C. Campbell and Percy A. Brown a committee ("Ways and Means Committee") to prepare a draft of the plan to be used for the guidance of the several communities in this matter.

In pursuance of a motion made by Dr. Walter Davis the Chairman appointed Dr. Davis, Dr. D. H. Lake, Dr. J. W. Geist and Miss Nellie G. Loftus a committee to report with respect to the systematic treatment of "flu" patients.

On motion of Wm. H. Conyngham it was voted: "(1) that an effort be made to retain here the five nurses who are now in this community, but who have been ordered to return to Washington on October 26; (2) that the Chairman of the General Committee communicate by telegraph with the proper officials at Washington, expressing our desire to have retained here, until the situation is improved, the army doctors who are now in the field, or that other doctors be sent to take their places, and that as many as can be furnished be sent."

On October 20, at a meeting of the General and District Chairmen, in conjunction with the members of the Ways and Means Committee, the latter presented a plan for the organization of outlying communities. This plan was forthwith adopted and ordered to be printed and distributed among the officials of the various communities.[4] Fuel Conservator Campbell reported that he had telegraphed to Federal Fuel Administrator Garfield, urging him to use his influence to have the army doctors then here kept here.

At this time the influenza and pneumonia conditions were "appalling" in certain localities in Luzerne County. At Glen Lyon, as well as at Georgetown in the township of Wilkes-Barre, the situation was very serious. An average of about 75 new cases per day in Wilkes-Barre was being reported, while all the emergency hospitals in the District were without sufficient help.

On October 22 new cases in Wilkes-Barre to the number of 120 were reported, while conditions in Glen Lyon, Nanticoke, Wanamie and some other places in the 5th District were "desperate". On this date Dr. Miner and the Chairman of the General Committee received the following communication, copies of which were immediately transmitted by them to the various emergency organizations in the 5th District.

"October 20, 1918. "From: The Commissioner of Health of Pennsylvania. "To: All concerned with Problem of Nursing during the present Epidemic of Influenza.

"Subject: Plan of Organization and Instructions. (General Order No. 2.)

"As it is not yet fully realized that the present epidemic afflicting us in these war times has caused the greatest need, and at the same time is accompanied by the greatest scarcity, of graduate nurses that has ever occurred, it is necessary to form a plan which may be adapted to any situation, as one community after another becomes involved:

"1. Graduate nurses must be used in such a way that their services be of assistance to the greatest number. This may be done by calling first upon all partially trained attendants, Red Cross workers, and then lay helpers, or any intelligent persons who are able to assist, and who will faithfully follow instructions. These latter must be instructed carefully in the essentials for treating patients, protecting themselves, and preventing the spread of infection, and be directed to make a simple record of their work each day, while the graduate nurses must move about rapidly to cover as much territory as possible if the cases are in private homes or in small groups, supervising the work of subordinates, instructing these subordinates, and following up their work. If the graduate is assigned to a hospital, the same plan should be used, i. e., nurses or lay helpers detailed to small groups of patients, with the graduate in charge. Thus an active graduate and subordinates who obey orders with military precision get actual results which cannot be obtained by attempts to furnish trained nurses to individual families or in quantity to hospitals.

"2. It is imperative that the lives and health of physicians, nurses and lay workers be conserved for service to the vast number afflicted. Accordingly in each hospital (emergency, tent-hospital or otherwise) or in each community which has been organized against the epidemic, a system should be devised to apportion the time and labor of all workers as equally as possible, according to the character of their work. All precautions against infection must be constantly observed, e. g., the wearing of gowns which cover the entire body; masks made by applying eight layers of surgical gauze, or two of butter cloth, to the convex surface of a wire tea-strainer about four inches in diameter, which is molded to fit the face from above the tip of the nose to below the point of the chin and secured to the head by tapes, (gauze changed every hour and boiled half an hour, sun dried and used over again); by the use of antiseptics, including careful cleansing of the hands after handling patients, before eating, etc., and care in destroying by burning or sterilizing infected material.

"3. Strict discipline (semi-military) is essential for saving time and insuring accuracy in receiving and executing orders. All persona! differences and likes and dislikes must be absolutely subordinated to the general need. Those in charge of others should exercise judgment in issuing orders to other subordinates, being careful to avoid anything which may be unnecessary or a repetition. Subordinates will observe instructions of their superiors without hesitation or argument. Courtesy at all times on the part of every one concerned will result in reaching most quickly the goal upon which our every effort is bent-the checking, if possible, of this great public disaster and minimizing its crippling effect and death toll.

"4. Requests for aid from stricken communities should be made to the nearest representative of the Department of Health, who will refer it to the Physician in charge of the Emergency District. This includes calls for doctors, nurses, aids, materials and any other form of relief. The Department will make a supreme effort to satisfy all such needs as rapidly as possible. However, where these are at hand they should be obtained locally.

"5. The best emergency hospital is the tent hospital, where the patient may obtain fresh air for twenty-four hours and receive sunlight by being hauled out into the company streets during the day. Wooden shacks or lean-tos (like those used in T. B. treatment), the walls of which may be raised by hinges and pulleys to admit the air and sunlight, are excellent. Buildings without balconies or porches should not be used unless there is adequate room or window space. Open air schools are almost ideal; next to them are modern high schools with large grounds about them. Visitors should be excluded, except relatives of dying patients, who should wear gowns and masks during the visit.

"6. Encourage the people of the community who wish to do something for the sufferers but cannot nurse them, to make masks, gowns and other supplies, also broths or other forms of nourishing food. Traveling kitchens or food delivered from a community kitchen by motor cars are of great assistance to stricken families. A County Committee should be formed for the purpose of investigating and promptly relieving distress, financial or otherwise. This committee could enable wage earners to remain at their employment.

"7. All existing agencies (local government, organizations, societies, orders, etc.) should be co-ordinated so that there be no uncertainty or confusion as to what is needed and how to meet the need and no waste of personnel or repetition of instructions or starts upon unnecessary errands.

"8. In each district, which may include several Counties, there is a physician in full charge of the district, with permanent headquarters. There is also a supervising nurse of the district, whose headquarters should be the same as the District Chief's, unless an emergency should make another arrangement desirable. All other Department officers are subordinates to these two representatives of the Medical and Nursing service respectively Reports by wire or 'phone are required daily at I p. m. from Supervising Nurse, District Chief, and from each County Inspector at the Epidemic Headquarters, Harrisburg. These officers should arrange that all of their subordinates in the district report to them at a convenient hour prior to this time.

"9. It should be borne in mind that the District Chief and Supervising Nurse of each district are responsible for their entire district and cannot be spared too long in any one locality. Their movements will depend upon exigencies which may arise and orders from this office.

"B. Franklin Royer.

"Acting Commissioner of Health."

On October 23 the eighth Emergency Hospital in the 5th District was opened in the Maffet Street School building at Plains, Luzerne County, with Miss May Conlon, Graduate Nurse, as chief nurse.

On October 25 the following-named United States Army medical officers, who had been on duty in the 5th District, returned, under orders, to Camp Crane: Lieut. C. F. Bahler, Lieut. Joseph Goldstone, Lieut. G. T. Meek and Lieut. J. A. M. Aspy. Capt. E. L. Hendricks, being ill at Hotel Sterling, remained here some days longer. Upon the above mentioned date General Dougherty, Chairman of the General Committee, telegraphed to Gen. Peyton C. March, Chief of Staff, U. S. A., as follows:

"By systematic organization and effort we have been endeavoring to combat Spanish Influenza in Luzerne County, with its population of 350,000 souls. We had 300 registered physicians in the County, of whom 115 have gone into the military service. We has over 12,000 cases [of influenza] in the County, and have established, in addition to the regular hospitals, seven emergency hospitals. But three medical officers of those who were sent here from Camp Crane now remain. Six thousand mine workers are ill with the disease, thus reducing the daily output of anthracite coal 15,000 tons, or at the rate of 300,000 tons per month. We are informed that you have 4,000 medical officers in training at Camp Greenleaf. We must have twenty-five physicians sent here at once. Please give us this number of physicians, as the spread of the disease is increasing, and we must have medical assistance. Our doctors are exhausted."

At a meeting of the General Committee held October 26 Chairman Dougherty reported that the Commissioners of Luzerne County had appropriated $25,000. to be used in defraying the expenses incurred in combating the epidemic in Luzerne County.[5] It was the general opinion of the members of the committee present that this money should not be distributed among the various communities entitled to it until the end of the epidemic. It was pointed out, however, that several communities had already made applications for needed funds. It was finally decided that a committee composed of the Chairman and three other members of the General Committee should prepare, and report at a subsequent meeting, a plan for the proper expenditure of the County appropriation.

Colonel Eyer reported on conditions at the Armory Emergency Hospital, and stated that many of the patients who had died there were practically in a dying condition when received into the hospital. At 9:20 o'clock P. M. the Committee adjourned and proceeded to the Lehigh Valley Railroad station, where the following-named United States Army medical officers were met upon their arrival from Camp Crane, Allentown, Pennsylvania, for epidemic work in Luzerne County, and were assigned to duty as herein noted.

Capt. H. W. Dessaussure (in command) and Lieuts. E. J. Burke, E. Z. Brunner, L. H. Hills and J. B. McGuinness, to report to Dr. J. W. Leckie at the Hazleton Emergency Hospital; Capts. E. B. Chenowith and Evan S. Evans, U. S. M. C, to the Wilkes Barre Armory Hospital; Lieuts. Robert Funston and A. C. Hall to report to Dr. Strieker at Nanticoke; Lieut. Frank F. Davis to report to Dr. Strieker for service at Glen Lyon; Lieut. Leroy Fredericks to report to Dr. Strieker for service at the Wanamie Emergency Hospital; Lieut. H. R. Lipscomb to be physician in charge at the Plains Emergency Hospital.

On this date, according to a report submitted by the County Medical Inspector to the State department of Health, the number of influenza and pneumonia patients undergoing treatment in the various hospitals in the 5th District were as follows: Hazleton Emergency, 22; Exeter

Emergency, 70; Dupont Emergency, 9; Wanamie Emergency, 55; Wilkes-Barre Armory Emergency, 46; Catawissa Emergency, 8; Plains Emergency, 19; Nanticoke Emergency, ?; Hazleton State, 75; Nesbitt West Side, 14; Wyoming Valley Homoeopathic, 15; Nanticoke State, 13; Mercy, 30; Wilkes-Barre City, 64; Bloomsburg, 19; Berwick, 26. (Riverside Hospital, Wilkes-Barre, had received no "flu" patients.)

On October 28 new cases in Luzerne County were reported as follows: Edwardsville, 40; Wilkes-Barre City, 98; Wilkes-Barre Township, 16; Larksville, 19; Plymouth Borough, 50; Plymouth Township, 12; Laflin, 10; Miners Mills, 29; Parsons, 18; Plains Township, 109; Ashley, 13; Hanover Township, 35; Laurel Run, 2; Sugar Notch, 2; Warrior Run, 19; Courtdale, 6; Dallas, 2; Dorranceton, 16; Forty Fort, 18; Luzerne, 31; Swoyerville, 16; Wyoming, 14; West Wyoming, 8; Avoca, 5; Duryea, 4; Dupont, I; Exeter Borough, i; Hughestown, 11; Pittston, 20; West Pittston, 4; Pittston Township, 4; Dorrance, 3 ; Kingston, 32; Hazleton, 27; Weston, 48; Conyngham Borough, 3; Freeland, 18; Lattimer, 11; St, John's, 1; Sandy Run, 11; Upper Lehigh, 6; West Hazleton, 72; Seybertsville, 2; Neuremburg, 22 ; Nanticoke, 64; Nescopeck, 3 —making a total of 956 new cases in Luzerne County.

On October 28 a joint-meeting of the General and Cooperation Committees was held in the rooms of the Wilkes-Barre Chamber of Commerce.

Chairman Brown stated that the biggest problem with which the Cooperation Committee had to deal was that respecting nurses. He further stated that something should be done immediately to establish organizations in those communities. He advocated more pay for nurses, and said he believed that a sufficient number of nurses could be secured, whereby better progress would be made in combating the scourge.

After some discussion it was voted that in Luzerne County the pay of graduate nurses should be fixed at $120 per month, and that of practical nurses at $75 per month. It was also voted that all nurses should be under the control of Miss Loftus and the General Committee.

It was decided to recommend the placarding of all homes in which influenza existed in all cities, boroughs and first-class townships in Luzerne County. Also, that all matters of publicity concerning the "flu" in Luzerne County should be handled by the Chairman of the Cooperation Committee.

Following the adjournment of this meeting the following "Publicity Bulletin" was issued.

"A meeting of all District Chairmen and members of the Ways and Means Committee was held this morning in the auditorium of the Chamber of Commerce. Reports received showed that in certain outlying boroughs and townships officials charged with the protection of the lives of their constituents, as well as the general heahh of their respective communities, are placing the lives of their people below their selfish aims by playing politics. It was decided that, unless the said officials take immediate steps to bring about proper organization and protection of their respective communities, action will be taken at once to have them removed and their places filled by people with a sense of honor, and who will give to their communities the protection to which they are entitled.

"It was also decided that there is a great need for field nurses, and that the sooner a sufficient number of such nurses can be secured, the sooner the epidemic will be checked in our community. It was decided to pay graduate nurses $120. per month and practical nurses $75. per month. All nurses will be in charge of Miss Nellie G. Loftus, who is stationed at the Wyoming Valley Dispensary, 184, South Washington Street, Wilkes Barre.

"It was also brought to the attention of the meeting that newspaper reports secured from people in boroughs and townships are not accurate, and that the same are an injustice to the said communities. In one community, where it was reported that thirteen deaths had occurred, correct figures show that the deaths numbered only three. Therefore, it was decided that the General Committee should be responsible for publicity given out only by the Chairman of the Cooperation Committee, to whom are sent all official reports from communities.

"It was also decided to recommend to the officials of all cities, boroughs and first class townships in Luzerne County the placarding of homes in which influenza exists.

[Signed] "Percy A. Brown,

"Chairman of the Cooperation Committee."

Reports to the Cooperation Committee on October 31 showed 709 new cases of influenza and 67 deaths theretofore unreported in forty-eight communities of Luzerne County-indicating a decrease in the number of new cases, but no decrease in the number of deaths.

On November 4 only seventy-three new cases in Wilkes-Barre were reported, and there were very gratifying indications that the scourge was subsiding in most parts of Luzerne County. It was estimated that 10,000 coal miners in the County were idle because of the "flu."

A well-attended meeting of the General Committee was held in the auditorium of the Wilkes-Barre Chamber of Commerce in the evening of November 6, with Chairman Dougherty presiding and Hayden Williams as Secretary. The County Medical Inspector, in reporting on conditions in his District, stated that Berwick in Columbia County and Plains in Luzerne County were still having a serious time with the epidemic. Nanticoke, he said, had also been hard hit. He stated that in Newport Township, Luzerne County, 249 people had died from the influenza. He declared that, while conditions in general were improved, new cases and deaths would likely continue to occur during the next three or four weeks.

The County Medical Inspector took advantage of this occasion to declare that too much could not be said about the good work accomplished by the general organization in Luzerne County, which had been the salvation of the entire County. Without it the loss of life would have been considerably greater, and many communities would have felt the full force of the epidemic. He then read a communication from the Acting Commissioner of Health, which he had received a short time previously, in part as follows:

"Where churches and schools have been closed during the epidemic of influenza, great care should be practised at the time of removing restrictions. Many children have been kept completely out of danger during this dangerous period, and to open too soon and run the chance of bringing them into contact with persons who have recently recovered, and who may perhaps be carriers, may again bring fresh outbreaks of the disease, particularly among school children.

"Then, too, thousands of public, private and parochial school-teachers have been actively engaged in nursing, and these teachers should have a few days of rest-preferably a week-and ought to be absent from work at the bedsides of the sick for that period of time before returning to the schools or to crowded services.

"I would urge that you take these things into consideration, and in conference with the School Boards arrange for resuming sessions, so far as possible, when two-thirds of the children in any school district are ready to return from homes where no one has suffered with influenza for a period of seven days. Where possible, medical or nursing supervision would be advisable-especially for a few days after opening the schools.

"I would suggest that, so far as practicable, the resumption of school work should take place about midweek, and of Churches and Sunday Schools on the Sunday following. This will bring children gradually together, and will avoid the overcrowding apt to occur in Sunday Schools if these schools were first opened. It is not necessary to tell you that fifty per cent, of the Sunday Schools are conducted in buildings not as well ventilated as are the public schools."

It was stated, in this connection, that over 2,000 school teachers throughout the State had been active in helping to fight the epidemic.

Upon motion of Percy A. Brown it was voted to publish the letter of the Acting Commissioner of Health, and to urge all school boards and Sunday Schools not to reopen their schools without first consulting the Boards of Health of their respective localities, to learn whether or not the resumption of school sessions would cause a further spread of the epidemic.

Chairman Dougherty, referring to the work of the various committees in this locality during the epidemic, stated that, while talking at Harrisburg a few days previously with Dr. Royer, the Acting Commissioner of Health, the latter informed him that the epidemic organization in Luzerne County was "the finest in the country, and the people of this County deserve great credit for the work done." General Dougherty then read a letter which he had just received from the Acting Commissioner, in part as follows:

"I am very greatly indebted to you for the splendid story of the Emergency hospitals, and to note what a tremendous amount of public interest your committee has aroused. It is only by such community service that it has been possible to save the number of lives of miners that we have saved during this public health drive. Too much credit cannot be given to your local committee, and I shall see to it that the press gives the local people a great share of credit."

Wm. C. Shepherd expressed the opinion that the General Committee should communicate to the various communities in the County the suggestions of the State Department of Health with reference to the lifting of the quarantine ban wherever it had been imposed.

Percy A. Brown, Chairman of the Cooperation Committee, reported that while the latest reports received showed there had been a general falling off of the disease, the daily average of new cases was about seven per district, compared with a recent average of ten per district. He stated that he expected to send out on the ensuing day, to every community chairman in Luzerne County, a questionnaire asking for certain information regarding the total number of cases and of deaths that had occurred since the beginning of the epidemic, together with a complete record of all workers, paid and volunteer. Later on, he said, he hoped to have a meeting of the various chairmen, with a view to forming an organization to prevent a recurrence of dangerous conditions during future epidemics.

County Controller Hendershot suggested that Chairman Brown's questionnaire should include a call for information with respect to the number of children orphaned by the epidemic. He said that if he could secure such information he would take it to Harrisburg and endeavor to secure additional aid from the State for the care of such children, He said he believed that the State would increase the Mothers' Pension Fund appropriation in order to handle such cases.

Wm. C. Shepherd declared that the gathering of various statistics, as proposed, would bring together valuable information for use in preparing for publication a history of the epidemic. These facts, in his judgment, should be printed and preserved for the benefit of future generations. In this connection the Rev. Father McCabe suggested that it would be wise not to take the census of the various communities until the epidemic was thoroughly stamped out. Dr. S. P. Mengel also stated that it would be unwise to take a census until the epidemic was over; and, as to the final data to be secured by a census, he said that only those facts furnished by the medical authorities should be accepted, inasmuch as no one else was competent to determine whether or not a person alleged to have been ill with influenza had suffered from that disease or something else.

The County Medical Inspector told of what had been done at Pottsville, Schuylkill County, towards taking care of the children made orphans by the epidemic. He also stated that he would like to see a community census taken, and a permanent record made of all persons who had helped in combating the epidemic in Luzerne County.

Dr. E. L. Meyers, a member of the School Board of the City of Wilkes-Barre, told of the good work performed by school teachers during the epidemic and in various public movements, and suggested that, when a census of community conditions should be made, the aid of school teachers and school superintendents should be enlisted in the work. He then offered the following resolution, which was unanimously adopted.

"Resolved, That the Chairman of the Cooperation Committee be instructed to appeal to the various school superintendents in Luzerne County for assistance in the making of a community census, for the purpose of ascertaining desired information in connection with the Influenza Epidemic, as well as for the protection of all communities against future epidemics. The questionnaire to be used by the school teachers in the making of the said census to be prepared by a committee of physicians to be named by the Chairman of the General Committee."

In pursuance of this resolution Chairman Dougherty appointed Drs. E. L. Meyers, S. P. Mengel, J. W. Geist and G. A. Clark a committee to prepare the proposed census questionnaire.

The Chairman then called attention to the necessity of devising a plan for the distribution of the money appropriated by Wilkes Barre City and Luzerne County for epidemic work. He called especial attention to the fact that it was not the intention of the General Committee to expend the money in a haphazard manner, but that only such bills as the respective communities should be properly relieved of would be paid. The greatest care should be exercised in arranging a plan that, when worked out, would give a square deal to all the communities and effect a general feeling of satisfaction.

Thereupon, on motion of Percy A. Brown, it was voted that the Chairman of the General Committee should name a committee to be known as the "Committee for the Distribution of Funds for the Care and Relief of Influenza Victims"; which committee should devise and carry out a plan for "the distribution of the funds provided for the expenses of emergency hospitals and the relief of victims of the Influenza Epidemic in Luzerne County."

It was further voted that this committee, before deciding upon a plan of distribution, should procure as much information as possible relative to the number of cases in each community, as well as the expenses incurred by the several communities.

In response to an inquiry made by the County Medical Inspector, it was decided that the rates of pay for nurses, agreed upon at the joint-meeting of the General and Cooperation Committees held on October 28, should, in each instance, run from the beginning of the nurse's service.

In pursuance of the action of this meeting Chairman Dougherty subsequently appointed the following-named gentlemen to compose the Committee for the Distribution of Funds. William H. Conyngham, Dr. Charles H. Miner, John O'Donnell, James M. Stack, Fuller R. Hendershot, Harry W. Ruggles, William J. Rufif, Percy A. Brown, William C. Shepherd and Gen. Charles B. Dougherty. At a later date the members of the committee met and organized by selecting William C. Shepherd Chairman, William J. Ruff Treasurer, and L. K. Eldridge Secretary.

On Thursday, November 7, the General Committee came to an understanding with the various municipal, school and Church authorities that it would be safe to re-open saloons and bar-rooms on Saturday, November 9, churches on Sunday, November 10 moving-picture houses, theaters, dance-halls, etc., on November II, Sunday Schools on November 17, and public, parochial and private schools (which had been closed on October 5) on November 18.

On November 5 the Catawissa Emergency Hospital (which had been established in a private residence) was closed. According to the final report received from the hospital there had been on the staff six physicians (including the chief), five Graduate Nurses and two orderhes. Thirty-nine patients had been admitted, of whom two died.

Hazleton Emergency Hospital was closed on November 8. The staff had consisted of two U. S. A. medical officers, five orderlies and enlisted men, one Graduate Nurse for five days, and a number of volunteer nurses-most of whom were school teachers. Dr. J. W. Leckie was in charge when the hospital closed. The total number of patients admitted to this hospital was 109, of which number 55 had pneumonia and 54 influenza. One influenza patient and forty-two pneumonia patients died — fourteen dying within twenty-four hours after their admission to the hospital.

Exeter Emergency Hospital was closed on November 11, at which time Dr. James Dixon was the physician in charge. There had been nine Graduate Nurses and three practical nurses on the staff, three volunteer nurses and, for a part of the time, three orderlies. Influenza patients to the number of 90 and pneumonia patients to the number of 79 (making a total of 169) were admitted, of which number 42 pneumonia patients died —13 dying within twenty-four hours after their admission to the hospital.

Nanticoke Emergency Hospital was closed on November 13, at which time Lieut. C. E. Yates, U. S. A., was the physician in charge, assisted by Miss Olwen Williams, Graduate Nurse. The staff had comprised four physicians (including the Chief), three medical officers, U. S. A., three Graduate Nurses, forty-three volunteer nurses, one medical student and seven orderlies.

Thirty influenza and 121 pneumonia cases had been admitted, and fortyone of the latter had died-fourteen dying within twenty-four hours after their admission to the hospital.

Wanamie Emergency Hospital was closed on November 14, at which time the physicians in charge were William H. Corrigan and Lieut. L. W. Frederick, U. S. A., assisted by W. R. Stewart, a medical student. Nine Graduate Nurses and five Practical Nurses (at different times), eleven volunteer nurses, thirty nurses' aids, thirty-one Sisters of Mercy, seven orderlies and one medical student were members of the staff at one time and another. Thirty influenza patients and 157 pneumonia patients were admitted to the hospital. Forty-nine of the latter died-twenty-one dying within twenty-four hours after their admission.

The Wilkes-Barre Armory Emergency Hospital was closed on November 14. As previously noted, this hospital was opened for the reception of patients on October 16, with the following staff: Capt. E. L. Hendricks, U. S. Marine Corps, physician in charge; Mrs. J. Pryor Williamson of Wilkes-Barre, a Graduate Nurse, as chief nurse; fifteen Graduate Nurses, nine aids and two civilian orderlies.[6]

The preparing and serving of food for the patients and the entire staff of the hospital were in the hands of the Red Cross Canteen service, under the capable direction of Mrs. E. Birney Carr. For the cooking and baking of the food the services of Mrs. P. J. Higgins were obtained, and under her expert directions the quality and quantity of food served were beyond criticism.

A system was early inaugurated for the purchasing of materials and supplies, under which system all materials and supplies needed, with the exception of food, were purchased by Lieut. Charles A. Trein (of the 2d Infantry, Pennsylvania Reserve Militia), acting as Purchasing Agent. Under this system accounts rendered were promptly approved by Col. S. E. W Eyer and ordered to be paid, with the confusion and no elaborate system of bookkeeping. With this system, and the cooperation of the medical officers and Graduate Nurses in charge, everything moved ?long with smoothness and regularity.

On October 24 Captain Hendricks was recalled to his unit at Camp Crane, Allentown, for oversea's duty. Unfortunately he was taken ill when about to leave Wilkes-Barre, and for three days thereafter was confined to his bed at the Hotel Sterling. On October 25 Lieut. Joseph Gooldstone, U. S. Marine Corps, was assigned to the Armory Hospital and remained in charge until October 31, when he, too, was recalled to Camp Crane to report for oversea's duty. Thus the hospital was deprived, for the second time, of a faithful, conscientious, tireless worker.

On October 28 Mrs. J. Pryor Williamson, a Red Cross worker in Wilkes-Barre on extended leave, who was serving as chief nurse at the Armory, was recalled to Washington. With her knowledge of hospital work, her energy and her untiring efforts, she had, in her twelve days of service at the Armory, placed the hospital upon a working basis which left no room for doubt as to her ability and good judgment with respect to the matters under her supervision. Mrs. Williamson was ably succeeded at the Armory by Miss Antoinette Schofield, Graduate Nurse, as nurse in charge, which position she held until the closing of the hospital.

On November 1 Capt. Evan S. Evans, U. S. M. C, was assigned to the hospital, and remained as physician in charge until November 14, when he, too, was recalled to Camp Crane. Captain Evans, with his sunny disposition and jovial smile, made many friends among the patients and others with whom he came in contact.

On November 14, with only three patients as inmates, it was decided to close the hospital. Therefore, two of the three patients were transferred to the City Hospital, and one was transferred to the Mercy Hospital. At that time an average of about thirty new cases of the pandemic were being reported each day in Wilkes-Barre. In consequence, the Armory Hospital was left intact for a period of about two weeks; but as, during that time, no new cases were received, the wards were dismantled and the building was fumigated and finally closed to the public on December 7.

All articles of food remaining on hand at the closing of the hospital were equally divided and donated to the Wilkes-Barre City Hospital, Mercy Hospital and the Wyoming Valley Homoeopathic Hospital. Other articles of use and value, after being properly fumigated, were turned over to the City of Wilkes-Barre authorities for use in the city's Hospital for Contagious Diseases, then in course of construction.

The total number of patients admitted to the Armory Emergency Hospital was 192, of which number 132 were males and 60 were females. Ninety-four of the patients were pneumonia cases, and of these sixty-six died. Three died from influenza. Thirty-five patients died within twenty-four hours after their admission to the hospital. The largest number of patients admitted in one day was eighteen-on October 17. The largest number of patients in the hospital on any one day was 62; the largest number of deaths on any one day was seven, and the largest number discharged on any one day was fourteen. Eighty-six of the patients were under thirty years of age.

Of the 192 patients received into the Armory Emergency Hospital 102 were from Wilkes-Barre; 20 from Edwardsville; 22 from Swoyerville; 7 from Ashley; 6 from Plymouth; 5 each from Kingston and Miners Mills; 4 each from Askam, Parsons and Forty Fort; 3 from Maltby; 2 each from Larksville, Sugar Notch, Nanticoke and Buttonwood; i each from Plainsville and Dorranceton.

The Plains Emergency Hospital was closed on November 18, at which time Lieut. H. R. Lipscomb, U. S. A., was the physician in charge, and Miss May Conlon, a Graduate Nurse, was the chief nurse. Five different physicians (not more than one at any given time) had served on the staff, together with four Graduate Nurses, three practical nurses, six volunteer nurses, one medical student, three orderlies and three enlisted men. Fifty patients were admitted (31 influenza cases, 18 pneumonia cases and one case of croup), and of this number thirteen of the pneumonia patients died-three of them within twenty-four hours after their admission to the hospital.

The Dupont Emergency Hospital was closed on December 3, at which time Dr. James S. Dixon was the physician in charge, and Miss Bessie Fadden, Graduate Nurse, was the chief nurse — she having succeeded Miss Herman on November 19. There had been on the staff four Graduate Nurses, five practical nurses (who worked part of the time), two sanitary detachments, and a number of Sisters of the Bernardine Order who served as volunteer nurses. One hundred and three patients were admitted to the hospital, of whom 83 were influenza and 20 were pneumonia cases. Twelve of the latter died-five of them within twentyfour hours after their admission to the hospital.

The following information, concerning influenza and pneumonia cases treated in some of the permanent hospitals located in the 5th District, has been derived from official reports made to the County Medical Inspector, covering the period from October 1, 1918, to January 1, 1919.

Wyoming Valley Homoeopathic Hospital: Total number of influenza cases, 68; pneumonia cases, 55; total number of deaths, 27.

Mercy Hospital: Total number of influenza cases, 133; pneumonia cases, 131; total number of deaths, 87 —including 22 who died within twenty-four hours after their admission to the hospital.

Wilkes-Barre City Hospital: Total number of cases, 457, comprising 223 influenza cases and 234 influenza-pneumonia cases. Two hundred and thirty-four of the number were male and 223 were female patients. The total number of deaths was 135. Of the members of the hospital staff, 72 contracted pneumonia at the hospital, and four of them died.

Pittston Hospital: Total number of influenza cases, 67 (males, 26; females, 41) ; pneumonia cases, 32, of which 13 terminated fatally.

State Hospital at Hazleton: Total number of influenza patients, 275; pneumonia patients, 216, of whom 113 died.

Berwick Hospital: Total number of influenza cases, 113; pneumonia cases, 25; total number of deaths, 16.

On November 18 the number of cases of influenza-pneumonia in Wilkes-Barre had increased to such an alarming degree that the municipal authorities imposed another quarantine ban, closing all amusement houses and prohibiting public assemblages. Eleven days later this ban was removed, although the daily average of new cases of influenza and pneumonia totaled about thirtyfive. The public schools of the city, however, having been closed about two months, were not re-opened until December 4, although at that time about eighteen new influenza cases a day were being reported in Wilkes-Barre. Conditions in other parts of the County seemed to be improving.

On December 15, owing to the large increase in the number of influenza cases in Wilkes-Barre, the municipal authorities ordered the closing of all schools except the City High School and private schools of a corresponding grade. Also, children under fourteen years of age were forbidden to attend theatres and motion-picture shows, to ride in pubHc conveyances and to visit stores. The sessions of Sunday Schools were also directed to be discontinued. The epidemic seemed to be particularly prevalent among children.

One hundred and four cases of influenza in Wilkes-Barre were reported on December 17, and the next day the municipal authorities imposed additional quarantine restrictions, the chief of which was that persons in quarantined houses-excepting physicians, and others given special permits-should not enter or leave such houses.

On December 19 the General Committee held a meeting, which was attended by the Health Officers of Wilkes-Barre, Dorranceton and Hanover. Chairman Brown of the Cooperation Committee reported that up to that date there had been 2,872 deaths from influenza and pneumonia in Luzerne County, 345 of which had occurred in Wilkes-Barre. The County Medical Inspector briefly outlined the situation in the County, and stated that in some cases officials were not reporting the true conditions in their localities.

At a meeting of the General Committee held on December 21 the County Medical Inspector stated that the conditions in the various communities in the 5th District were such that the Acting Commissioner of the State Department of Health was not inclined to order any further quarantine ban, unless requested to do so by the authorities of the respective communities. Dr. Clark, of the Bureau of Health of Wilkes-Barre, reported that the situation in the city during the last four days had been better than for some time previously-only 35 new cases having been reported. He said that so far in the month 1,020 cases had been reported, while in November only 825 cases had been reported. More children and fewer adults were being attacked by the disease.

Mayor Kosek stated that he was averse to crippling the business of the community, but he felt that everything possible should be done to stamp out the epidemic. He said he was in favor of giving the matter considerable publicity, and urged that officials in the outlying communities should be asked to cooperate with the city authorities in the enforcement of regulations.

Resolutions were then adopted to the effect that any further plan for fighting the epidemic, which should be adopted, should be enforced vigorously until all danger had passed; that places of amusement should be closed to children; that public funerals and overcrowding at public gatherings should be prevented. The following resolution, offered by Dr. S. P. Mengel, was then unanimously adopted:

"Resolved, That this committee endorses the rules and regulations adopted by the Board of Health of the City of Wilkes-Barre, and that we ask for the strict enforcement of the same, and that we pledge cooperation in aiding the authorities to bring about such enforcement; and further, that we call upon the entire public, as well as the officials of all communities in Luzerne County, for their cooperation in reducing the number of cases of influenza by obeying to the letter all rules and regulations adopted by the Wilkes-Barre Board of Health; and we also ask the cooperation of every newspaper in Luzerne County in bringing this matter to the attention of the people."

On December 23 Mayor Kosek of Wilkes-Barre made an official announcement to the people of the city, to the effect that, if they would not voluntarily observe the reasonable quarantine regulations which had been adopted by the city authorities, he would impose a quarantine that would be the most far-reaching and absolute that had yet been ordered, and this without regard to what interests might be thereby affected.

At this time the officers of the Bureau of Health of the city were firmly opposed to the lifting of the ban with respect to public dances, cabarets, Sunday School sessions, and other public assemblages during the approaching holiday season. However, about the first of January, 1919, the ban against moving-picture houses was lifted, and on the 10th of the month the remaining restrictions of the quarantine were removed, and Sunday Schools and the public and private schools of the city resumed their sessions.

The following table, compiled from official records and reports, indicates the total number of known cases of influenza and pneumonia, and the total number of deaths therefrom, that occurred in Luzerne County from October 1, 1918, to January 1, 1919.

Community	Total Cases	Total Deaths	Community	Total Cases	Total Deaths
Ashley Borough	391	43	Parsons Borough	575	49
Fairview Twp.	150	8	Plymouth Boro. and		
Avoca Borough	250	26	Plymouth Twp.	1,559	95
Courtdale Borough	32	8	Shickshinny Borough	275	25
Conyngham	300	42	Sugar Notch Borough	450	22
Dallas Borough	25	5	Wright Twp.	13	0
Dorranceton Borough			Dorrance Twp.	62	4
(including Westmoor)	357	80	Swoyerville Boro.	2,000	81
Duryea Borough	704	65	Warrior Run Borough	132	15
Edwardsville Borough	600	121	West Hazleton Boro.	479	53
Exeter Borough	950	120	West Pittston Boro.	685	53
Forty Fort Borough	138	14	Exeter Twp.		1
Freeland Boro. and			West Wyoming Boro.	144	22
Foster Twp.	1,567	104	White Haven Borough	182	3
Hughestown Borough	160	7	Wyoming Borough	325	30
Jeddo Borough	471	18	Yatesville Borough	0	0
Kingston Borough	660	68	Hazleton	3,012	338
Kingston Twp.	25	4	Hazle Twp.	790	77
Laflin Borough	84	0	Butler Twp.	74	6
Larksville Borough	594	82	Pittston, Pittston Twp.		
Laurel Run Boro.	150	4	and Jenkins Twp.	1,366	261
Luzerne Borough	520	44	Wilkes-Barre	4,817	521
Pringle Twp.	157	14	Wilkes-Barre Twp.	531	60
Miners Mills Borough	546	40	Bear Creek Twp.	5	2
Nanticoke Borough	1,772	299	Plains Twp.	1,620	133
Slocum Twp.	63	6	Bucks Twp.	0	0
Hanover Twp.	359	46	Nuangola Borough	0	0
Newport Twp.	3,700	192			
Nescopeck Twp.	165	17	Grand totals	34,043	3,332
New Columbus Borough	30	4			

Total number of children made orphans in Luzerne County............2,390

The following table sets forth the number of cases of influenza and pneumonia treated, and the number of deaths occurring, in the Emergency Hospitals in Luzerne County:

The following detailed statement indicates very clearly the character and amount of the work done for nurses and patients by the members of the Red Cross Canteen of Wyoming Valley Chapter during the pandemic:

Number of quarts of soup distributed.......October 2,158
November 3,946
December 2,456

Total 8,560

Number of quarts of milk distributed.......October 50
November 560
December 805

Total 1,415

Number of lunches packed for nurses........October 532
November 917
December 203

Total 1,652

Number of quarts of lemon syrup served.....October 20
November 18

Total 38

Number of quarts of lemon jelly served.....October 51
November 40

Total 91

Number of quarts of pineapple juice served..October 2
November 2

Total 4

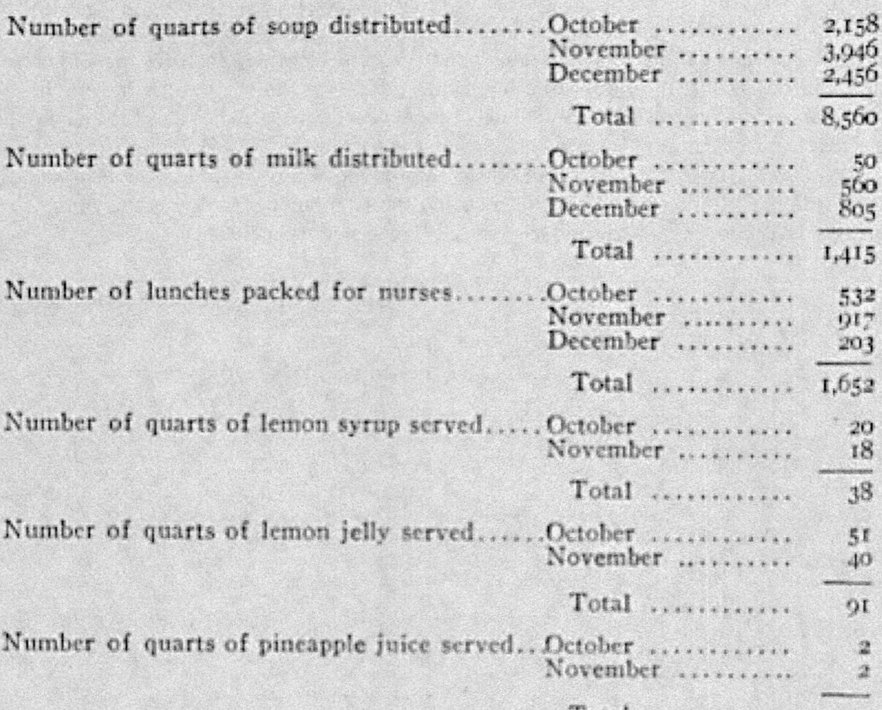

Desserts were distributed in which the following articles were used:

Article	Unit	Qty	Article	Unit	Qty
Milk	qts.	2,013	Peaches	can	1
Gelatin	qts.	295	Cocoa	boxes	4
Eggs	doz.	335	Junket Tablets	boxes	2
Lemons	doz.	42½	Cornstarch	boxes	155
Rice	lbs.	15	Tapioca	boxes	141
Vanilla	qts.	9	Gelatin	boxes	202
Grape Juice	bottles	4	Lemon Jello	boxes	12
Raspberry Juice	bottle	1	Sugar	lbs.	316
Pineapple	cans	4	Ice Cream	qts.	56

Vegetables used in soup.......October ....qts. 40
November ....qts. 40
December ....qts. 40

Total (approx.) qts. 120

Rice used in soup.......October ....lbs. 26
November ....lbs. 40
December ....lbs. 50

Total (approx.) lbs. 116

Barley used in soup.......October ....lbs. 10
November ....lbs. 3
December ....lbs. 10

Total (approx.) lbs. 23

Soup was distributed in Wilkes-Barre and outlying districts, and was sent to the Visiting Nurses' rooms and to the Home for Friendless Children. Corresponding amounts of desserts were sent out in Wilkes-Barre, and outlying districts, and to the Home for Friendless Children. Jellies and marmalades were donated in large quantities, and were sent out with the soup and desserts. The sum of $500.00 was donated for free milk for influenza patients.

Although Troop Trains were being served during the month of December, the Canteen continued the work incidental to the epidemic. From Canteen Headquarters large quantities of soup, custards and milk were distributed to individuals and families in the city and outskirts. Three thousand nine hundred and seventy-four people were served. Two thousand four hundred and fifty-six quarts of soup were distributed; 167 quarts, with corresponding quantities of custard, were sent to Georgetown, and 13½ quarts to the Visiting Nurses' rooms for their lunches. Eight hundred and five quarts of milk were distributed. Two hundred and three lunches were packed for volunteer nurses on duty in the stricken homes. Twenty-four quarts of ice cream were distributed on Christmas Day. Desserts were distributed in which the following were used: 739 quarts milk, 84 quarts gelatin, 117½ dozen eggs, 10½ dozen lemons, 4 quarts vanilla, 47 boxes cornstarch, 53 boxes tapioca, 33 boxes gelatin, 12 boxes lemon jello, 85 pounds sugar.

At a meeting of the Greater Wilkes-Barre Chamber of Commerce held December 10, 1918, with President Philip R. Bevan in the chair and Hayden Williams Secretary, a very full discussion took place with respect to the large number of children in Luzerne County who had been orphaned by the influenza scourge (2,390, as noted on page —, ante)—creating a condition demanding the serious consideration of every citizen of the County. Thereupon the following resolution was adopted:

"Resolved, That a committee be appointed to look into this matter, and make recommendations at a subsequent meeting of the Chamber."

Pursuant to this resolution President Bevan appointed a committee as follows: William C. Shepherd, Chairman, Percy A. Brown, C. F. Brisbin, John N. Conyngham, Charles E. Clift, William H. Conyngham, Fuller R. Hendershot and John D. Farnham. This committee met on January 3, 1919, and after careful deliberation unanimously decided that, before any consideration could be given to a definite plan for the permanent relief of influenza orphans, it would be necessary to form a general committee drawn from various sections of the County of Luzerne. Chairman Shepherd declared that, whatever plan of relief should be adopted, it should apply to the entire County. He said, also, that it would have to be decided whether or not any of the children could be taken care of by existing charitable organizations, or whether a special institution would have to be established.

Mr. Hendershot, and others present, raised the question as to whether or not any of the children could be taken care of by the Mothers' Pension Fund. It was admitted that if this were done the appropriations for the Fund would have to be increased. It was stated that, as there were some Counties in the State which did not have such a Fund, the local Board might be able to secure an increase in its appropriations from the State funds not drawn upon by other Counties entitled thereto.

Mr. Brisbin told of the investigation then going on by members of the Red Cross, and others, under his direction, in order to ascertain all conditions surrounding each individual affected by the ravages of the pandemic. He said that when the inquiries should be completed, in the course of two or three weeks, there would be definite information as to the exact number of orphans for whom permanent provision would have to be made. He said that in many cases orphans would either be placed in the care of relatives, or others, and that in the end the number to be provided for by the public would not be as large as then anticipated.

It was then resolved, upon motion of Mr. Brown, that a committee, representative of the entire County, should be appointed: "To devise plans for the permanent relief of all influenza orphans needing the same; and that prior to a meeting of this General Committee to be held on January 20, 1919, the Secretary should communicate with the various cities in Pennsylvania and other States, in which the epidemic had been serious, for the purpose of securing information regarding permanent relief plans adopted in those cities."

In pursuance of this resolve it was decided that the following named persons should be invited to come together at the Chamber of Commerce on January 20, 1919, at 3 o'clock P. M., for the purpose of effecting a "permanent organization for the relief of influenza orphans in Luzerne County." William C. Shepherd, Percy A. Brown, C. F. Brisbin, William H. Conyngham, John N. Conyngham, John D. Farnham, Hon. S. J. Strauss, Hon. J. V. Kosek, Miss Anna Koons, Charles F. Huber, Miss Mary Brady, Miss Rose O'Hara, Dr. Charles H. Miner, Dr. S. P. Mengel, Eugene W. Mulligan, Anthony C. Campbell, Mrs. George Galland, Mrs. Francis A. Phelps, Mrs. Andrew F. Derr, Miss Hobart, Miss Nellie Ritchie, Mrs. J. D. Davenport, Victor Lee Dodson, Frederick J. Weckesser and Harold N. Rust of WilkesBarre; Michael Lonski, F. H. Kohlbraker, Mrs. George G. Brader and Mrs. Oliver Bell of Nanticoke; Fuller R. Hendershot, Dr. H. L. Whitney, H. L. Freeman, Michael Maras and the Hon. Asa K. De Witt of Plymouth; Mayor Henry W. Heidenreich and Harry A. Schmoll of Hazleton; Wilham Bray of Freeland; D. A. Mulherin of Glen Lyon; the Rev. M. A. Dauber of Pike's Creek; Robert Mulhall, William Joseph Peck, M. N. Donnelly, Mayor James Kennedy, M. W. O'Boyle, W. L. Watson, W. J. Kilgallen and Mrs. Joseph Peck of Pittston; Samuel M. Parke of West Pittston; Mrs. E. E. Buckman, Mrs. Laurance M. Thompson and Harry W. Ruggles of Dorranceton; the Rev. F. Kasaczun of Sugar Notch; V. B. Sheeder and the Rev. Mr. Gillespie of Wanamie; the Rev. Selden L. Haynes, the Rev. J. F. JedHcka and Hubbard B. Payne of Kingston; the Rev. J. E. Gryczka of Edwardsville; James L. Reilly, Secretary of the Poor Board of the Central District of Luzerne County.

In response to notices sent out to the aforementioned persons, about thirty-five of them assembled in the auditorium of the Wilkes-Barre Chamber of Commerce in the afternoon of January 20, 1919. At the request of Chairman Shepherd Mr. John N. Conyngham acted as Chairman pro tern. Mr. Shepherd then explained the purpose of the meeting, and the necessity for providing some satisfactory method of taking care of the children throughout the County who had been left in a destitute condition by the influenza pandemic.

The Chairman pro tern, asked whether or not a permanent organization should be formed. Mr. Mulhall thought that it would be wise to work through some organization already in existence and possessing power to enforce any law relating to the situation. He suggested the United Charities as such an organization, and supplementary to this suggestion Mr. Schmoll reported that in Hazleton forty-six influenza orphans were at that time being taken care of by the United Charities of that City.

Mrs. Galland, President of the Mothers' Pension Fund, thought it would be the best plan to leave as many children as possible with their surviving parents, and that practically all cases could be handled by the Pension Fund-provided appropriations for it should be sufficiently increased.

On motion of the Rev. Mr. Haynes it was finally voted that a temporary organization be formed, to be known as the "Chamber of Commerce Cooperation Committee", to cooperate with existing agencies in making investigations and providing relief for all deserving cases.

Mr. Brisbin, Chairman of the Civilian Relief Department of the Wyoming Valley Chapter of the Red Cross, stated that his department had begun investigations, regardless of any arrangements made, or to be made, by other committees or organizations. It had been stated that the Women's Committee of the Council of National Defense was about to institute an investigation of the orphan problem along the same lines being followed by the Red Cross, and Mr. Brisbin called attention to the danger of serious confusion and complications as a result of this overlapping work.

Mrs. Phelps and Miss Brady (the latter an employee of the United Charities of Wilkes-Barre) spoke of conditions found by them in many homes where poverty reigned, and where it was necessary that something should be done immediately to save these families from being ejected from their homes by landlords because they could not pay their rents. Thereupon Mr. Mulhall inquired why the Poor Boards could not pay the rents of families in destitute circumstances.

Mr. Dodson said that while the Poor Board of the Central District was publicly not in favor of paying rents, he believed it would take care of the rent question quietly by paying money for that purpose to the United Charities. Mr. Farnham stated that the Red Cross had some money which might be used for that purpose.

Upon motion of Mr. Hendershot it was then voted that a committee be appointed to work in conjunction with the State Department of Health in an attempt to secure from the State Legislature financial relief for all influenza orphans. As such committee the Chairman appointed Fuller R. Hendershot, John D. Farnham and Percy A. Brown.

Upon motion of Mr. Haynes it was then voted to adjourn until January 22, at which time efforts would be made to devise an immediate plan for the permanent relief of influenza victims; and that the Secretary should invite to this meeting representatives of the Red Cross, the United Charities, and the Poor Boards in Luzerne and Carbon Counties.

The adjourned meeting of the Chamber of Commerce Cooperation Committee held on January 22, 1919, was attended by about twenty persons. Mr. William C. Shepherd presided, and L. K. Eldridge acted as Secretary. Mr. Shepherd stated that it was the consensus of opinion that, so far as possible, all orphans should be kept in their respective homes or be taken care of by relatives or friends. Mr. Brisbin outlined the work being done by the Civilian Relief Department of the Red Cross, stating that cases were being investigated, and that in his judgment the County had organizations enough to take care of the work, but that money was greatly needed.

Thereupon Mr. Hendershot moved that a committee be appointed to confer with the Poor Board, the Red Cross and other organizations with a view to obtaining money for carrying on the relief work. This motion having been carried the Chairman appointed the following committee, to be known as the "Ways and Means Committee": William H. Conyngham (Chairman), Dr. Charles H. Miner, Anthony C. Campbell, Harold N. Rust and the Rev. Selden L. Haynes.

Charles E. Keck, Esq., Solicitor for the Poor Board of the Central District, then outlined the duties and limitations of that Board, and stated that the members of the Board would be very glad to meet the committee just appointed and go over with them the matter of providing funds for needed relief. At this point Judge S. J. Strauss made some very timely remarks to the effect that a committee should be appointed to provide means for increasing the capacity and usefulness of the Wilkes-Barre Home for Friendless Children. He stated that, in his opinion, additional organizations were not necessary, but that the Committee should co-operate with those already existing.

At a meeting of the Chamber of Commerce Cooperation Committee held on January 31, 1919, Mr, Rust, reporting for the Ways and Means Committee, stated that the latter had conferred with the attorney for the Poor Board of the Central District, who informed the committee that in any case where immediate relief was required the Board would investigate and then administer such relief as was necessary.

Mr. Rust was of the opinion that, inasmuch as the taxpayers had provided funds for the Poor Board, action should be taken by this Committee to see that the Board properly took care of worthy cases. Further, that as the law of the State prohibits the paying of rents by the Board, the matter of rents should be taken care of by the Red Cross; that there should be close cooperation between Wyoming Valley Chapter of the Red Cross and the Poor Board of the Central District in the matter of investigating cases; that immediate relief, when needed, should be furnished, and that the disbursement of funds should be divided between the Poor Board and the Red Cross. Mr. Farnham stated that in his opinion the funds of the Red Cross would be available as far as they would go.

On motion of Mr. Rust it was then voted that the Civilian Relief Department of Wyoming Valley Chapter of the Red Cross take to the Poor Board of the Central District the fifty specific cases which they had investigated; that these cases should be checked up against those receiving relief from the Central Poor District, and if it should be ascertained that there were any who were not receiving relief, the District be requested to add such names to their list for immediate investigation and relief; that the District pay for food, coal, etc., and that funds for the payment of rents be placed in the hands of the Civilian Relief Department of the Red Cross.

On motion of Mrs. George Galland it was voted that the Cooperation Committee of the Chamber of Commerce endorses the action of the Commissioners of Luzerne County in agreeing to appropriate $25,000 to the Mothers' Pension Fund provided the State of Pennsylvania would appropriate $1,000,000 to the general fund.

A meeting of the Cooperation Committee of the Chamber of Commerce was held on February 19, 1919, with William C. Shepherd presiding and L. K. Eldridge acting as Secretary. The minutes of the meeting held on January 31 were read and approved. Mr. Rust reported concerning the conference held by the Ways and Means Committee with the Poor Board of the Central District, stating that the latter had agreed to carry out, so far as possible, the recommendations set forth in the resolution of the Cooperation Committee adopted on January 31. The support promised by the Poor Board would cover medical assistance, food, clothing, and nursing when necessary; the Red Cross to pay rents.

Mrs. McLaughlin reported that the original fifty relief cases had been turned over to the Poor Board, together with 202 additional cases. The Poor Board had stated that 90% of these cases were already in their hands, under investigation. It was also reported that several day nurseries were under consideration, which would permit mothers to leave their children there and take up employment. Mrs. Phelps stated that in a number of cases widows had not yet received their insurance money; that some of the societies in which insurance had been carried were said to be bankrupt, while some of the larger insurance companies were holding up the payment of amounts due on policies of deceased victims of the epidemic.

On motion of Mr. Rust Mr. Brisbin was authorized to increase the membership of the Civilian Relief Committee so as to meet the requirements of the situation of affairs. It was voted, also, that he be given full power to discuss and decide all matters with the Central Poor Board, and that he consider the wisdom of employing persons to do social service work during the ensuing three months.

On April 30, 1919, a quorum of the Chamber of Commerce Cooperation Committee met in the Chamber of Commerce auditorium. Chairman Shepherd stated that, inasmuch as the Red Cross and the Poor Board of the Central District were taking care of matters for which the Cooperation Committee had been constituted, it was his judgment that the Committee should be discharged from further consideration of the matters in question. Mr. Schmoll stated that in Hazleton all cases had been taken care of through regular channels, and to the best of his knowledge there were no destitute cases at that time. Mrs. Bell reported that in Nanticoke there were twelve cases where rents were being paid, and would be paid as long as necessary, by the Red Cross.

Mr. Conyngham stated that the work of the Red Cross, at that time, was confined to the paying of rents. He could not say, however, how much longer this work could be continued. It was suggested that, when the Red Cross had reached the limits in its work of paying rents, the Poor Board should take over the cases in Nanticoke. Mrs. McLaughlin stated that up to that date 630 old cases and 75 new ones in the Central District had been turned over to the Poor Board.

On motion of Mr. Conyngham it was voted to request the Poor Board to employ as many experienced women as necessary to investigate and look after cases after the Red Cross and other organizations had retired from activity in the field. The Rev. Dr. Farr suggested that the Cooperation Committee should receive from Mr. Brisbin a full and final report of the important work done by the Civilian Relief Committee of Wyoming Valley Chapter of the Red Cross, which work had been carried on under the direction and management of Mr. Brisbin, and has been briefly referred to hereinbefore. There being no further business to be transacted, the Committee adjourned sine die.

The "Committee for the Distribution of Funds for the Care and Relkef of Influenza Victims", whose appointment is noted hereinbefore, held various meetings for the transaction of business connected with the duties confided to it. At a meeting held March 21, 1919, affairs relative to the various Emergency Hospitals were thoroughly discussed, following which Mr. Conyngham moved that all bills of the General Committee be paid at once. This motion was carried. Mr. Hendershot then moved that the Treasurer be instructed to pay the amounts of the various Emergency Hospital bills which had been approved by the Committee. This motion was carried.

At a subsequent meeting this Committee unanimously adopted the following rules of procedure relative to the settlement of bills arising out of the establishing of the seven Emergency Hospitals in Luzerne County:

"(1) That the verified bills for the construction work of buildings, or altering or equipping temporary hospitals, should be paid.

"(2) That the verified bills for the daily maintenance-consisting of food, drugs, medicines, and the overhead expense of light and fuel together with such special expenses as were approved by the General Committee in relation to the general organization work throughout the County, be approved and paid.

"(3) That bills in connection with the regularly established hospitals, and bills relating to the regular hospitals and charities, and the work of attendants in isolated homes, could not be approved and paid, as the moneys appropriated for this epidemic were appropriated for the specific purpose of the establishment and maintenance of hospitals for this work."

At a meeting of the Distribution Committee held April 4, 1919, it was resolved to issue to the public a "Letter of information concerning the work of the Distribution Committee". This letter was subsequently prepared, giving a brief account of the organization of the committee and the work it had accomplished, and, having been signed by the members of the committee, was duly disseminated. The following paragraphs are extracts from this letter:

"The appropriation of funds by Luzerne County was made under an Act of the Pennsylvania Legislature approved May 14, 1915, and reading in part as follows:

"'Section 1 * * * The County Commissioners of any County may appropriate moneys for the support of any hospital, located within or without the limits of such County, which is engaged in charitable work and extends treatment and medical attention to residents of such County.

" 'Section 2. All Acts and parts of Acts inconsistent with this Act are repealed.'

"The appropriation of the City of Wilkes-Barre was made by the members of the City Council by a resolution reading as follows:

" 'Whereas, the equipment and maintenance of the Emergency Hospital at the Armory is necessary to fight the influenza epidemic; and whereas much of the equipment can be later used at the Emergency Contagious Disease Hospital of the city of Wilkes-Barre which is now nearing completion.

"'Therefore, Be it Resolved, That the City of Wilkes-Barre appropriate $5,000., or so much thereof as may be necessary, toward the equipment and maintenance of the Armory or other Hospital; that the Citizens' Committee in charge submit bills, properly audited, to the City of Wilkes Barre, and the City pay such bills to an amount equal to the appropriation authorized; and that the equipment, which can later be used by the Emergency Contagious Hospital, become the property of the City; and that patients at the Armory Hospital, whose circumstances permit, be required to pay for such services, as is done at the other hospitals in the City.'"

DISTRIBUTION COMMITTEE INFLUENZA EPIDEMIC.

RECEIPTS.

From Luzerne County	$20,000.00
City of Wilkes-Barre	3,999.85
Wyoming Valley Chapter Red Cross	3,963.36
The Bell Telephone Company (Refund)	14.76
H. A. Whiteman & Co. (Refund)	38.45
	$28,016.42

EXPENDITURES.

Paid to Nurses, Aids, etc., as follows:

Emily Jones	$ 40.00	Beth Porter	47.52
Hilda Lewis	40.00	Margaret Larkin	47.52
Nellie Loftus	40.00	Ada Bachstein	34.57
Jennie May	40.00	Dorothy Tennyson	39.46
Minnie Fry	40.00	Edna Bachstein	26.23
Mrs. Harriet Hountz	54.00	Eleanor Brown	26.23
Loretta Sullivan	102.00	Mrs. E. Silvara	40.00
Anna Walsh	80.00	Irene Lewis	40.00
Dorothy Guy	85.50	Ruth Rae	40.00
Nellie Fischer	7.33	Lida Tucker	50.00
Margaret Bechtold	84.00	Margaret Burns	37.29
Oliver Wolfe	108.00	Rose Costello	47.33
Raymond Davis	51.00	May Williams	62.00
Howard Roat	75.00	Clara Campbell	20.00
Robert Davenport	36.00	Emily Sprake	5.50
Mrs. Martha Edwards	48.63	Mrs. P. Hanson	80.83
Mrs. Myrtle Mooney	14.52	Jessie Cunningham	14.00
Mrs. Ellen Hosey	45.53	Leslie Covert	42.00
Bessie Evans	7.26	George Berry	57.00
Hazle Smith	7.26	Ernest Wright	6.00
Lenore Williams	42.92	Mrs. Margaret Jacobs	19.02
Evelyn Jones	15.97	Elizabeth Williams	15.97
Gwyn Winters	41.32	Anna McNulty	81.29
Goldie Womelsdorf	39.97	Florence Desh	11.61
May Conlon	56.23	Mrs. Lena Krum	7.26
Nellie Sheridan	29.47	Margaret Griesmer	44.23
Katherine Dymond	32.52	Ellen McGuigan	54.73
Mrs. Hilda Hogg	45.87	Olwen Williams	41.32
Mary Sinko	23.61	Kathleen Bishop	10.16
Bessie Fadden	66.77	Mrs. Jean Langford	29.42
Esther Lynn	55.16	Gertrude Lenahan	20.32
Laura Hughes	57.82	Mildred Perry	50.32
Annette Schofield	31.35	Madge Heffron	47.56
Susan Sable	43.16	Mary Roache	2.00
Sister Angela	35.42	Alice Fuller	43.06
Ethel Jordon	31.35	Mrs. James Lockett	11.61
Sarah Wilson	7.46	Leyl VanHoesen	1.46
Arline Hale	10.50	Mrs. F. T. Mitchell	31.16
Helen Wheatley	33.00	Anna Boyle	7.40
Katherine Longshore	40.81	Sister Pierre	41.23
Ruth Jones	47.52	Anna McMenanin	23.06
Verda Vivian	39.46	Olive Carle	4.35

Name	Amount	Name	Amount
Jeanette Washington	7.50	Nan Wintersteen	25.35
Alice McCarty	18.00	Mrs. Kate Heston	1.01
Irene McGinty	10.50	Mrs. E. Roszykiewicz	0.08
Margaret Andes	40.81	Anna Owen	6.67
Ellen Davis	47.53	Mrs. Marie Caffrey	13.29
Mary Humphrey	47.52	Jennie Audi	16.48
Margaret Porter	47.52	Nora Aubrey	16.15
Agnes Riley	39.46	Mrs. Mollie Dennison	18.29
Mable Davis	24.19	Kathleen Lavelle	59.68
Katherine Gaffikin	47.52	Helen Slacinski	60.27
Mildred Weathers	47.48	Josephine Rookry	34.09
Anna Tobias	50.00	Margaret Meekin	95.16
Maria Blazick	54.84	Anna Groschke	50.50
Irma Goodale	56.39	Sarah Kelley	25.81
Catherine Thomas	59.08	Mary Clemmons	21.66
Ann Shaughnessy	13.35	Marie Strome	27.58
Mrs. G. L. Todd	46.51	Iona Brelsford	16.13
Anna Yanalovitch	85.48	Doris Reedy	75.81
Mary Koseck	82.26	Mrs. A. Dowling	31.62
Millie Heslop	88.71	Mayette Mulligan	52.85
Eleanor Martin	66.13	Helen Mais	23.12
Mrs. Ann Davies	15.00	Marjorie Lindsay	49.25
Helen Yablonski	29.09	Alice Kochinsky	12.90
Anna Eaton	67.20	Sophia Roach	68.87
Edith Franklin	56.46	Edna Runyan	45.54
Mary Mieczkoski	69.93	Jennie Moore	11.29
Margaret Burke	47.00	Elizabeth Morris	22.58
Freda Turner	19.52	Ruth Thomas	22.58
Hannah Davis	17.06	Annette Kivler	.81
Ethel Jones	47.52	Laura Kokensperger	23.06
Emma Cleason	33.87	Violet Clark	5.65
Carolina Bryant	22.58	Mrs. Mary McClusky	4.94
Leah Craig	33.87	Martha Howard	22.53
Marguerite Davey	33.87	Blanche Wilkes	33.87
Bertha Griffith	33.87	Mary Levix	11.29
Mrs. Kathleen Brew	30.90	Mary Biezrak	22.58
Nell Jordan	19.84	Sophia Chukinski	23.13
Beatrice Sorber	28.03	Helen Gajewski	16.67
Nellie Blackburn	33.87	Myrtle Socha	41.67
Helen Finley	33.87	Sarah Taff	49.57
Barbara Swanberry	28.98	Mrs. Hannah Jones	22.02
Elizabeth Breunas	11.29	Mrs. Delia Dunn	11.67
Margaret McDonald	37.74	Mrs. Maria Jones	24.17
Jennie Jesuit	16.67	Mrs. Margaret Jones	10.83
Frances Keller	16.67	Mrs. Margaret Meehans	11.67
Mrs. J. Bavrick	46.51	Mrs. A. Steinhauer	43.55
Mrs. E. Massman	26.19	Mrs. C. Devaney	3.23
Mrs. Blanche Evans	41.94	Mrs. C. Davies	4.03
Mrs. Clara Swishere	.81	Mrs. Minnie Llewelyn	22.06
Emma Wagner	12.50	Mrs. Marie Shaffer	8.36
Rachael King	11.67	Gertrude Cooper	22.06
Mrs. Ellen Dailey	28.88	Mrs. Anna Norris	27.04
Mrs. Ruth Tyrell	25.38	Mrs. Minnie Reich	20.95
Mrs. Elizabeth Deitrick	31.07	Mrs. Esther Hogg	14.94
Kathryn Kransky	23.77	Mrs. B. Mulhern	28.23
Mrs. Minnie Williams	22.15	Mrs. Charles Burk	3.33
Elena Heineman	28.73	Mrs. Belle Connor	5.83
Gertrude McCarthy	39.52	Mrs. M. Farber	13.15
			——————
			$6,746.34

Footnotes

1.   This arrangement provided accommodations for sixty patients, which, later on were found to be insufficient to meet the demands for admission to the hospital' whereupon four more wards of the same dimensions and materials were erected. These wards, when completed, gave the hospital eight wards with a total capacity of 120 beds. Of these eight wards six were used for patients in general as admitted one was used as an isolation ward (where patients in the last stage of pneumonia were placed), and one was used as a ward for convalescents.

2.   At this time the regular, or permanently established, hospitals located in the 5th District were as follows: Wilkes-Barre City, Mercy, Wyoming Valley Homceopathic and Riverside Hospitals in Wilkes-Barre; Nesbitt West Side Hospital Dorranceton; Pittston Hospital, Pittston; Berwick Hospital, Berwick, Columbia County State Hospital of the Middle Coal Fie'd of Pennsylvania, Hazleton; Stsilte Hospital' Nanticoke; Bloomsburg Hospital, Bloomsburg, Columbia County.

3.   In pursuance of this suggestion a six-page leaflet was subsequently prepared and printed in English, Italian and three other languages, and was well distributed throughout the District.

4.   This was subsequently done, in the following form: PLAN OF COMMUNITY ORGANIZATION FOR THE EPIDEMIC EMERGENCY. 1. Community Chairman (President of Board of Health). 2. Executive Committee, consisting of: A. Board of Health. B. Burgess and member of Borough or Township Council. C. Mine Superintendent and representative of labor union. D. Principal of schools. E. Red Cross Worker. F. Member of Council of National Defense. G. Clergyman. H. Prominent Citizen. I. Local Physician-principally in advisory capacity. 3. Secretary. 4. Emergency Station. 5. Community Captains. 6. Nursing Bureau. 7. Canteen Service. 8. Automobile Service. 9. Publicity Bureau. 10. Miscellaneous.

5.   About this time the City Council of Wilkes-Barre made a special appropriation of $s,ooo. to be used in fighting the "flu" in the city. This sum was in addition to the regular annual appropriation for the city's Bureau of Health.

6.   During the existence of the hospital the total number of physicians (including the Chief) on the staff was five; the number of Graduate Nurses was fifteen; the number of volunteer nurses was twelve (three Graduates and nine aids); the number of orderlies was ten, and of enlisted men, fifteen.